To Shoheed
I notice you during
my speech. I could.
see that you were activating
yourself success. You can
create whatever you want.
Phillip Clem
11/20/91

THE
POWER
TO
CREATE

THE POWER TO CREATE

PHILLIP AARON

Pennington Publishing
Dallas

Pennington Publishing, 2525 Rosebud Court, Carrollton, TX 75006

Printed in the United States of America
95 94 93 92   5 4 3 2 1

ISBN 0-9630418-0-0
Edited by Kathryn P. Ingley
Cover Designed by John Watson

To Theresa Aaron, my daughter,
who is a real self-actualizer;
to Richard, my son,
who has the virtue of patience
and the gift of creativity;
and to P. J., my youngest son,
who acknowledges no defeats
or barriers.

"If you follow your bliss, you put yourself on a kind of track that has been there all the while, waiting for you, and the life that you ought to be living is the one that you are living. Wherever you are—if you are following your bliss, you are enjoying a refreshment, that life within you, all the time."

—Joseph Campbell
The Power of Myth

CONTENTS

Two

Learning to Empower Your Goal

THE POWER TO CREATE

PREFACE

About ten days after my seventeenth birthday, I was arrested when police officers stopped a car in which I was riding and which, I later discovered, had been stolen. I spent 72 hours in jail while police investigators took their time in determining that I had, in fact, not been involved in anything illegal. To the contrary, I was simply in the wrong place at the wrong time. This experience was the most traumatic, painful, and jarring that I have had, before or since.

When I look back now to those 72 hours, I realize that *The Power to Create* principles were really conceived then. For it was there, in that jail cell, as a 17-year-old youth, that I made up my mind to do whatever I needed to do to ensure that I would never again be in such a position. I wish I could say that I decided to become an attorney at that time, but the truth is I only decided never to go to jail again. The decision to become an attorney came much later.

The only other immediate decision I made was to leave St. Louis, Missouri, and set myself on a course toward a life that would provide me with mental, intellectual and economic tools to ensure that I could protect myself and those for whom I was concerned. So at 17, I dropped out of high school and enlisted in the United States Air Force with the definite intention of completing high school and at least starting on a college education.

But when I got to Yokota Air Force Base in Japan, I underwent another traumatic experience that proved to be both painful and a major turning point in my life, one that added another cornerstone to the principles upon which this book is based. I was seated in a recreational room in a large barrack on the base, and several people in the room were discussing some current event. I said something and there was dead silence, then laughter. To this day I do not remember what I said, but I remember the hurt and the embarrassment I felt. I left that room and, as I walked back toward mine, I decided that I would read a book a week until I had educated myself to a point where I could engage in a conversation without being subjected to that type of response.

One of the first books that helped me to control my life was Maxwell Maltz's *Psycho-Cybernetics*. With the principles of psycho-cybernetics and some other things that I read on hypnosis, positive thinking, and the like, I began to shape my life. This shaping eventually led to my receiving a law degree from the University of Washington. Six months after I graduated from law school I opened my own practice, focusing primarily on trials. I practiced law for about 15 years, during which time, I also owned a garbage disposal company and a commuter airline.

By then, I had developed the principles on which this book is based, but my adaptation of them was sporadic. I believe this, to a large part, is because I used to drink a lot. From the time I was 15 years old until several years ago, I had not gone more than a month without consuming a fairly large amount of alcohol, perhaps as a sort of rebellion against my strict religious background. In my sobriety, I came to realize the power of the inner core that I had developed, beginning in that jail cell, and I began to place these principles into action. Since then, my goal has been to grow into my full self and to inspire and help others to grow into themselves.

Let me hasten to say that you don't have to have the difficult background that I've got to benefit from these principles. In fact, I hope that you don't. One of my primary motivations for writing this book—in fact, my mission in life—is to show you that it is not necessary for you to step on the same jagged rocks I have stepped on. If I can tell you where those rocks are so that you can avoid stepping on them, I can make a major contribution to your life. In turn, you can do the same for me and for others.

The Power to Create has grown out of the life journey that I have briefly described. I have tested these principles in the laboratory of life, and I can assure you that if you adhere to them on a consistent basis, you will experience a richer, fuller life.

This book is about how you can have that richer, fuller life. It is a book about change for the betterment. It is designed to lead you to self-discovery and to the embracement of your True Purpose, your True Talent, and your True Goal. "If you want something you have never had," someone once said, "you must be willing to do something you have never done."

It is urgent that you do this now because there is so little time left. According to statistics, most people today will live 70 to 75 years. From this, you can see how little and how precious the time you have left really is. When you understand that time stands still for no one, then you know that you must make the most out of your life right now.

The statement that time stands still for no one captures the essence of life, because no matter what we do, whether it is good or bad, productive or unproductive, or directed toward a goal or ill-directed, time moves on.

It has moved on in your own life. Look at the things you wanted to do in the past ten years that you haven't done. If you assume that you would take the same attitude in the future as you have in the past, and if you project that attitude ten years out, then you can see how unproductive your life will be if you let things remain the way they are now. I'm sure that ten years ago you had dreams and important plans that you wanted to accomplish by this age: maybe you wanted to become rich, own your home, own your own business, succeed at your profession. Your intentions were sincere, but you put things off and somehow time just seemed to slip away, and before you knew it, ten years had passed.

If you look closely, I think you will find that you simply put things off until tomorrow. But those things you put off were some of the most important things in your life: your health, your prosperity, your success, your relationships.

Like the rest of us, you forgot that tomorrow is an illusion. Tomorrow is incomprehensible and we cannot experience it, because the only time we can live is today. We never really know if there will be a tomorrow, yet we act as though we have all the tomorrows we want; we put things off as though we control tomorrow, yet there is nothing more uncertain. How long you or I will live—how many tomorrows we will see—is anybody's guess. We all know that tomorrow is not promised, yet most of us live as though it were.

If you want to maximize your life and eliminate procrastination, forget tomorrow and live on the premise that today is all you have. Once you have accepted that fact, you will begin to live your life with the direction and the gusto with which it is meant to be lived. Time stands still for no one, but today you can start living the life you ought to be living and capture its full beauty.

You are about to embark on the discovery of what that life is, but, remember this, the life you ought to be living is one that is unique and personal to you. The purpose of this book is not to identify what your life is to be, but to lead you along the path of self-discovery so that you can find and determine for yourself the kind of life you ought to be living. What you find when you get there is not within my control, and, in fact, is not really my focus. My objective is to lead you to self-discovery and to encourage and to congratulate you for having discovered whatever it is you find.

One final word: I'm writing this book to you. Although I understand and appreciate the need to recognize and acknowledge both genders, I find it extremely awkward to have to say "he or she" in those situations which require third person singular constructions. Upon my editor's advice, I have chosen to use the traditional "he." I trust that you will understand that this choice will facilitate the smoother flow of my thoughts.

Phillip Aaron

ACKNOWLEDGEMENTS

Thanks to the people at Context who helped me to grow into myself, and to my family, friends, and educators.

A special thanks to Beth Hanford whose labor, honest critique and genuine support were immeasurable.

Thanks to my son, Phillip Richard Aaron, for his creativity, help and patience. And to my 10-year-old son, P. J. Aaron, who always helps me realize the beauty of living my purpose in life. And thanks to my daughter, Theresa Aaron, who is a living example of self-actualization and who is my favorite critic. If she likes something, I know it's okay.

INTRODUCTION

I congratulate you for taking this major step toward self-discovery and the identification of the unique life you ought to be living. I cannot guarantee that you will find any particular thing, but I can assure you that with a reasonable level of participation and openness you will lay aside this book with the skills, knowledge and internal state that will enable you to create and achieve exactly what you want.

Before we get into the substance of the book, let me share with you some things about its structure, in terms of its content and presentation. The book is divided into four sections. Section 1, Tapping Your Inner Power, is the foundation of the book, and in it you will identify your True Purpose, your True Talent, and your True Goal.

Section 2, Learning to Empower Your Goal, deals with the principles and rules of empowering and bringing life and vitality to your goals. In other words, you will learn how to develop a sensory-rich goal statement and how to create the internal state that empowers.

Section 3 combines the concepts of Section 1 and the principles of Section 2, and is called Empowering Your Personal Goals. In this section, you will apply the principles you have learned to your True Purpose, your True Talent and your True Goal.

Section 4, Developing Your Personal Success Script, deals with bringing your conscious and subconscious mind into harmony in reference to your True Talent, True Goal, and True Purpose.

Upon completion of this book, you will have the internal state necessary to create exactly what you want; you will have a self-talk script that enriches and brings your subconscious and conscious mind into harmony with your goals; and you will have the basic knowledge of how to use these tools to their optimum.

This book also deals with some other tools with which you are already familiar: goal-setting, affirmation and visualization. Many books and tapes purport to teach you how to be successful, and most of them tell you how to set goals, how to write affirmations, and how to visualize the outcome. If your experiences have been like mine, you were initially excited by these courses, but after awhile your enthusiasm waned. We certainly cannot conclude from these experiences that goal-setting, affirmation, and visualization are not important to success. The most we can conclude is that something else must be needed to get from desire to actualization of desire, or to accomplish what you want.

This book is designed to bridge that gap. You will learn skills that have three important characteristics: They will be simple, effective and practical. And you can integrate these skills into your normal everyday life in a way that is easy and natural for you.

Think for a moment how important that is. I can remember reading self-improvement books and listening to tapes—and I've read and listened to many—all of which purported to lay out some sort of magical method of reaching goals. Some of the books were very good, and some were not so good. I remember going through one series of tapes that required me to set 30-day goals, 6-month goals, 1-year goals, 5-year goals, 10-year goals, 15-year goals and 20-year goals. Then the course required me to develop a plan leading to each of those goals, and to develop alternate steps in case I ran into obstacles along the way. I attempted to go through the program, and by the time I had finished, I had sketched out what I thought were my life's plans. I had the drafts, the circles, the blocks, and everything else. But I was confused and totally frustrated because I was left with a maze of ill-defined, disconnected and undirected dreams.

If you have been unfortunate enough to have had a similar experience, relax because this is not one of those books. There is no need to make life, or your life's plans, difficult and incomprehensible. Life is not meant to be that way. So in this book, you will find clarity and simplicity. You will learn how to reach that reservoir of power within you. You will learn to identify and commit to your True Purpose, and from there to develop your True Talent so that you can achieve your True Goal.

The best way to learn and to develop new skills is to use them and to adapt them to your particular activities. That is why the information in this book is designed to get you involved. It will work best if you will let the text and exercises, which are designed to build one upon the other, lead you to self-discovery.

You can benefit from this book without doing the exercises, but to get the maximum benefit, it is important that you be willing to do them from the core of your being, responding openly and honestly. In that regard, let me suggest that you and I make a pact to help you get around any inhibition or reluctance that would prevent your doing them. You will be doing nothing in these exercises that is embarrassing, belittling, or uncomfortable in any sense. No response is too silly, no questions are too bad, nothing is unacceptable within the reasonable, moral and ethical bounds of these exercises. It is important that you do the exercises in a way that is meaningful and beneficial to you, and that your responses be from your core because you are trying to reach your true essence. To do this requires that you be open and honest, sometimes painfully so.

ONE
TAPPING YOUR INNER POWER

IDENTIFYING YOUR TRUE PURPOSE

Living your True Purpose is the answer to life's frustrations because then you are being what you ought to be and occupying that space that is uniquely yours. Living your True Purpose is what Abraham Maslow, the eminent psychologist, called self-actualization.

Maslow believed that there are two basic types of human motivation: 1) deficiency motivation which includes such things as oxygen, food and water, and 2) growth motivation which includes striving for knowledge and self-actualization. According to his theory, motivation is based on a hierarchy of fulfillment, beginning with satisfying first the basic physiological needs (oxygen, food, water) followed by safety needs, belonging and love needs, esteem needs and finally the need of self-actualization, which he defined as developing and fulfilling one's innate, positive potentialities. To illustrate his position, he named such eminent historical persons as Abraham Lincoln, Thomas Jefferson, Albert Einstein, Eleanor Roosevelt, and William James as self-actualizers.

Self-Actualization

In order to give empirical support to his position, Maslow sought out people who appeared to him to be self-actualizing persons. He interviewed a large number of people and selected those who seemed to have full use of their talents, capacities, and potentialities—people we would call high achievers.

In studying these high achievers, Maslow observed several consistent factors and patterns among them such as the following: they efficiently perceived reality and were comfortable with it; they accepted themselves and others; they had deep feelings of identification, sympathy and affection for human beings in general; they were spontaneous and appreciative; they had deeper and more profound relationships and were capable of more bonding and greater love than most people; they manifested a sense of humor; they were creative; they were more concerned with end results than with methodology; they resisted enculturation (while not especially unconventional, they were relatively independent of their culture); while not being loners, they appreciated their privacy; they were autonomous—active, responsible, self-disciplined, deciding agents rather than pawns of others. As a result of his studies, Maslow concluded that above all else, self-actualizing people were devoted to something outside of and larger than themselves. He also found that self-actualizers worked at something that brought them immense joy and that was precious to them. In his book *The Farther Reaches of Human Nature*, Maslow says:

> They are working at something which fate has called them
> to somehow and which they work at and which they love,
> so that work-joy dichotomy in them disappears.

He concluded that a self-actualizing person is on a journey of self-growth. He then identified eight behaviors which lead to self-actualization.

First, live in the present as an active participator rather than a passive observer. Or, to put it another way, be focused. Maslow said the self-actualizing person experiences life "fully, vividly, selflessly, with full concentration and total absorption..."

We have all experienced being totally focused on participating in the moment. One such experience that is common to most of us is that of sexual union in which one becomes totally absorbed and loses consciousness of self in order to fully experience and participate in the moment of gratification.

I remember another experience from my trial practice during which I was totally focused and absorbed. I was defending a deranged 15-year-old youth who was charged with first degree murder and was being tried as an adult. I had been practicing law for only a couple of years and this was my first major trial. When time came for my final argument, I realized that the outcome of the case depended heavily on the speech I would give the jury. Apprehensive and somewhat nervous because of the weight of this responsibility, I decided that I knew all the facts of the case and that I had to trust myself, so laying aside my prepared speech, I surrendered fully to the moment. For that brief period, I became so absorbed in my argument that I truly lost consciousness of myself. The result was a hung jury—even though he admitted to murder. To this day, I look back on that experience with awe—I was so alive! Only one other time have I experienced that aliveness in my trial practice, but I have experienced it several times in other areas of my life.

Second, choose growth rather than fear or defenses. Growth choices lead you to become a better you. You choose to be honest rather than to lie, to give rather than to take, to love rather than to hate, to earn rather than to steal, to go rather than to stay, to change careers or businesses, associates, or relationships. The list of choices is endless. In essence, the self-actualizing person always chooses growth.

The more I focus on my True Purpose, the more I find myself choosing growth. One such choice was truly a leap of faith. I was involved in a partnership with three distinguished gentlemen, but the relationship was not beneficial to me. On the one hand, I was honored to be associated with them because of their perceived social stature, but on the other, their personal approach to me was less than what I wanted and expected. Finally, I realized that the cost to my self-esteem greatly outweighed any benefit I got from associating with them, and I severed our ties. Immediately, I experienced a freedom and a clarity that are hard to describe. This clarity enabled me to see that my bad experience was due to choices I had made, rather than anything they had done.

Third, look for the self within and actualize it. Maslow taught that the process of self-actualization "implies that there is a self to be actualized." By this self, he meant that essence at the core of your being—the real you—that you find when you peel back the layers of your life as you would peel an onion. You can reach your optimal self within—that best-you-can-be self—by opening your heart and mind to it.

Usually, people learn to open their hearts to the self within as a result of some dramatic, life-changing experience. They seem to discover this inner essence quite by accident. This is especially true of those who are not purposefully involved in the process of self-actualization. In *Think and Grow Rich*, Napoleon Hill gives several examples of how tragedy helped bring forward the optimal self in some of history's greatest players. He points out that John Bunyan and O. Henry became great authors after being imprisoned, and that Charles Dickens produced several masterpieces after a tragedy in his personal life.

I have tremendous respect for Gordon Graham, a 20th century man who took tragedy and turned it completely around. Gordon spent 17 years in prison, including a year in solitary confinement where he existed on bread and water. He escaped and was later imprisoned again. He was stabbed and he was shot. His prison experience was painful, but, I imagine, the pain was heightened by the fact that subconsciously Gordon knew what he could accomplish and how much good he could bring this world if he let his optimal self emerge. Through these tragic experiences, Gordon looked for and found his optimal self. Today, he is an author and one of the most sought after lecturers, consultants, and educators in the field of self-actualization.

And finally, we have all heard about the almost supernatural experience Martin Luther King, Jr., had when he was doubting his role in what was to become the major movement of this century. He was experiencing so much fear and doubt that he was ready to turn the leadership over to older and more experienced activists. In *Let the Trumpet Sound*, Stephen B. Oates tells of the threatening phone calls, the insults, jeers, and profanities hurled at King during the days of the boycott. Some callers threatened to not only murder King, but to kill his wife and daughter too. Then a friend reported from reliable sources that an assassination plan was afoot. King admitted that he was paralyzed by fear, but all the same he found himself at mass meetings trying to give the impression of strength.

Then late one night, exhausted from a Montgomery Improvement Association (MIA) meeting, he answered the phone and "an ugly voice...cut through King like a dagger, 'Nigger, if you aren't out of this town in three days we gonna blow your brains out and blow up your house.'" Unable to go back to sleep, King walked the floor, afraid and alone.

He put his head in his hands and bowed over the table. "Oh Lord," he prayed aloud, "I'm down here trying to do what is right. But, Lord, I must confess that I'm weak now. I'm afraid. The people are looking to me for leadership, and if I stand before them without strength and courage, they too will falter. I am at the end of my powers. I have nothing left. I can't face it alone."

He sat there, his head still bowed in his hands, tears burning his eyes. But then he felt something—a presence, a stirring in himself. And it seemed that an inner voice was speaking to him with quiet assurance: "Martin Luther, stand up for righteousness. Stand up for justice. Stand up for truth. And, lo, I will be with you even unto the end of the world." He saw lightning flash. He heard thunder roar. It was the voice of Jesus telling him still to fight on. And "he promised never to leave me, never to leave me alone. No, never alone, No, never alone. He promised never to leave me, never to leave me alone. . . ."

King raised his head and strength flowed through his being. He could face his task. "Whatever happened, God in His wisdom meant it to be. King's trembling stopped, and he felt an inner calm he had never experienced before. He realized that 'I can stand up without fear. I can face anything.'"

In each of these men, the other self which lay just below the surface emerged when tragedy jolted, or circumstances forced, or when the man himself called it forth.

Fourth, accept the responsibility for self-actualization. Responsibility here involves looking to yourself, or within yourself, for answers. It means having the courage to explore your being and the honesty to see and examine what you find there. Instead of viewing yourself as a victim whose life is controlled by others and who can only react to their choices, you accept responsibility for your life and shape it according to your own dreams and purposes. Taking the responsibility for self-actualization is, perhaps, the most liberating experience you can have.

When Gordon Graham stopped seeing others as the cause of his condition and took the responsibility for his life, he began to change in ways that were nearly miraculous. The acceptance of accountability empowered both his character and his life; he became what Joseph Campbell calls a hero. According to Campbell, a hero is a person who "learns to experience the supernormal range of human spiritual life and then comes back with a message." Gordon's message is about changing lives for the better, and it is directed to both the corporate world and the "consumers of correctional services." His own experience with the services propelled him to a level of awareness, concern, and understanding that enabled him to bring a real life-changing message back to those whose lives have gone astray.

Fifth, stand courageously in your self-actualization. History is ripe with examples of people who have dared to be different, to go against the norm of the day. Abraham Lincoln, Mahatma Ghandi, Martin Luther King, Jr., and Nelson Mandela all dared to listen to their inner voices and to trust what they heard. And each had the courage to make an honest statement about where he stood.

Nelson Mandela, a young African lawyer whose father was a tribal chief, courageously led the black protest against the white-minority government of South Africa and its rigid policy of racial segregation. His accountability cost him dearly—he was charged with treason and other serious crimes; he had to go into hiding; he was convicted of sabotage and conspiracy and sentenced to life imprisonment—yet he firmly stood on his convictions that racial segregation was wrong and, in 1990, he was released from prison.

Sixth, actualize your potentialities constantly. In *The Farther Reaches of Human Nature*, Maslow says that self-actualization is not only an end state, but also the process of actualizing one's potentialities at any time, in any amount. It means working at being the best in your field. It means being first rate instead of second rate. You can, for example, become smarter by studying, because self-actualization is also the process of using your intelligence. To be self-actualized you do not necessarily have to do some far-out thing, but you probably will have to go through arduous and demanding preparation in order to be first rate. No pianist likes doing the finger exercises, but those hours spent at the keyboard lead to self-actualization as a pianist. Self-actualization means working to be the best you can be in your chosen field. You cannot be second rate and be self-actualized.

Seventh, seize moments of joy and ecstasy on a frequent basis. Maslow believes these moments of joy are part of discovering yourself, and he calls them peak experiences. In his terms, these are experiences of happiness, fulfillment, and being. For him, this experience of being was a temporary, nonstriving, non-self-centered, purposeless, self-validating end experience; it was a state of perfection and goal attainment. He believed peak experiences are the results of a myriad of things, such as:

- Breaking up an illusion
- Getting rid of a false notion
- Learning what your talents are
- Learning what potentialities you lack

Eighth, identify your defenses and find the courage to give them up. Or in the words of Maslow, ". . . finding out who one is, what he is, what he likes, what he doesn't like, what is good for him and what is bad, where he is going and what his mission is. . . . It means identifying defenses, and after defenses have been identified, it means finding the courage to give them up."

Self-actualization leads you away from your defenses to your inner power, enabling you to create your own future and to be the best that you can be. Self-actualization is success in its operative form. When you have reached self-actualization, you will be living your True Purpose and have a fulfilled life where:

1. Work and play merge.
2. Life becomes easy in those areas where you are actualized.
3. The world sees the same "you" that resides at your core.
4. Honesty dominates your life.
5. Adventure fills your life; you explore beyond your present situation, seeking to grow.
6. Courage undergirds your personality.
7. You are devoted to something beyond yourself.

Self-actualization, or living your True Purpose, involves growing into your potential by preparing to become first rate at whatever you choose and by moving toward being the best you can be. It involves leading a fulfilled, successful life in which you create your own future. To promise all this seems to offer too much. But the fact is, this promise is absolutely true.

Each principle, when placed in totality with others, transforms your thinking and helps you create the life you want to live. In the following pages, you will explore eight of these principles and you will see how each relates to your creative ability.

- Self-Talk
- Beliefs
- Structural Tension
- Reticular Activating System (RAS)
- Self-Efficacy
- Accountability
- Comfort Zone
- Completion

Self-Talk

Self-talk is your narration of reality, the "facts"—words, thoughts, feelings, impressions—that you constantly store in your subconscious mind. Your success or failure at everything is tied to these facts because, whether true or not, your mind believes what you tell it. And what you tell it about yourself, it will create. It cannot help it.

So your self-talk creates your reality. It creates either a reality that supports your self-actualization or one that does not. Your reality and your facts may differ totally from another person's, because from childhood, you have been sifting, sorting, analyzing, judging, cataloging and storing everything that goes on around you. And each new fact is tied to one you already have placed into your subconscious.

When you observe something, you do so with all of your five senses. But you do not record the event, you record your *interpretation* of the event. Your self-talk interprets what you see, hear, feel, taste, or touch and informs your subconscious and, although not always, it informs your conscious mind. This interpretation defines your perception of reality.

Fortunately, you have the ability to control your self-talk and make it work for your benefit. All that is required is for you to develop a new, more nurturing script and to discipline yourself, initially at least, to play it in your mind. In Section 4, I will show you how to develop this script and how to implement it in an easy, almost effortless, manner. But for now, I want to show you how self-talk determines your reality.

Suppose, for a moment, that you wanted to start a wholesale jewelry manufacturing business and that you needed to buy some diamonds. Since you have little experience in the jewelry business, it is natural that your guard would be up and that you would be alert to anyone's trying to take advantage of your inexperience. When you approach a diamond seller, he is careful to explain each detail, sometimes simple ones, to you. He shows you a small, flawless diamond, and then he shows you a larger one of lesser quality. As he shows you these stones, he points out that you must not get duped by size. Through self-talk, you tell yourself that the diamond seller somehow knows that you are a rookie and that his explanations are really a con game to get you to buy the smaller diamonds at an inflated price. So you buy the larger one, only to find, after you have set it in its mounting, that no retailer will buy it from you. You learn your lesson about flawed diamonds, but you also conclude that all diamond sellers are dishonest.

From the standpoint of your personal reality, it does not matter that this particular diamond seller had shown good, honest motives and had, indeed, been instructive, because you have judged, based on your self-talk and resultant experience, all diamond sellers as dishonest. You will, consequently, act accordingly, and each time you deal with a diamond seller in the future, you will play your don't-trust-him-he's-a-crook script.

You talk to yourself all the time, but most of it is at a subconscious level. Self-talk pervades every moment of your life; you never stop talking to yourself. More than 50,000 thoughts go through your mind each day. When you are left to your own thoughts, your rate of self-talk is about 8 times faster than normal conversation. But when someone else is talking to you, self-talk slows to 3 or 4 times faster than the person is speaking.

Self-talk takes on various forms: words, thoughts, feelings, impressions, insights, flashes of intuition, or physical responses such as butterflies in the stomach, a pain in the gut, or a headache. All this information—what you are constantly telling yourself—is stored in your subconscious mind and from there it dictates your perception of reality and your responses to both the world around you and your inner world.

To control your reality, and hence your world, you must control your self-talk. This is the first and indispensable rule of creating your own future. While it may not be easy at first, controlling self-talk will soon become second nature and effortless once you start living your True Purpose.

Self-Talk and True Purpose

Changing your self-talk initially requires some purposeful actions, such as:

- Listening to your own self-talk
- Listening to the self-talk of others by observing the results
- Keeping a record of your negative self-talk
- Keeping a record of your positive self-talk
- Identifying both positive and negative external influences

As you discover and actively live your True Purpose, your self-talk will change naturally toward supporting this purpose. This process is, in part, what Maslow is talking about in *Motivation and Personality* when he says that "the distinction between coping and expression, like so many other psychological dichotomies, is resolved and transcended, and trying becomes a path to not trying."

Once you embrace your True Purpose, or become self-actualizing, you will become absorbed with it in every respect, and you will find there simply is no room for negative self-talk. It is impossible to truly embrace your True Purpose and to sabotage yourself with negative self-talk; the two actions cannot exist simultaneously. They simply cannot occupy the same space. But initially, as you begin to live your life purpose, you must consciously observe and direct your self-talk. The following two exercises will help you control your self-talk.

Self-Talk Exercise

Keep a 30-day True Purpose Journal, with a section for daily self-talk analysis. I have included formats for both the negative and the positive exercises of this section, together with some examples of how to complete the analysis.

Look first at the negative Daily Self-Talk Analysis chart below. Under the column entitled "Negative Self-Talk," list all of the negative, non-supporting self-talk or thoughts that you have had today.

In the second column, entitled "Harm to Me," list how this negative self-talk harmed you or how it created obstacles to your embracing your True Purpose.

In the third column, entitled "Rescripting," write affirmations that will replace your negative self-talk and support your True Purpose.

Daily Self-Talk Analysis
Negative

Negative Self-Talk	Harm to Me	Rescripting
I'm just not creative.	Creates a mental block.	I am creative.
That's just my luck.	Reduces expectations.	I make my own opportunities.

Now look at the positive Daily Self-Talk Analysis chart that follows. In the first column, entitled "Positive Self-Talk," list your self-talk that supports and embraces your True Purpose.

In the second column, entitled "Aided Me," record how this self-talk aided you.

In the third column, entitled "Comments," make a few notes to yourself about your observations, feelings, and the results of your positive self-talk.

Daily Self-Talk Analysis

Positive

Positive Self-Talk	Aided Me	Comments
I can do it.	Increased Expectations.	I started looking for ways to do the task
I'm a winner	Re-focused thinking.	I felt greater self-confidence.

Your Thoughts/Comments:

As I said earlier, these two exercises will help you take control of your self-talk. Try them for 30 days and you will be amazed at the difference in your life.

Beliefs

Your self-talk determines your beliefs, and your beliefs dictate your actions and responses. Here is how it happens: From childhood, your self-talk has supplied information about yourself and the world around you to your subconscious mind, which then turned this information into beliefs, without regard to whether it was true or false. In fact, your subconscious mind does not require something to be true; it only requires that you *believe* it to be true. This repeated self-talk convinces your mind that the information is true and then your mind forms your beliefs.

Your beliefs are your "facts." They are the screen through which you view the world. If you believe the world is hostile, you will see hostility, animosity and hate. If, on the other hand, you believe it is friendly, you will see warmth, cooperation and friendliness. The amazing thing is that you can find evidence to support either perception of your environment.

Beliefs are powerful. Once formed, they take root and function automatically to ensure that your actions agree with them. As an example of how powerful beliefs can be, look at the European world of the 15th century. Before Christopher Columbus, many people believed that the world was flat, and because of that belief no one would sail beyond a certain point. Consequently, most of the beauty of the world was unknown to the Europeans. Was this erroneous information a fact in the minds of the people? Not only was it a fact to them, but they considered it to be *truth*. It was their reality. Not until Columbus sailed west to reach the east and discovered the new world, did they recognize that their belief was untrue. The reality of their world changed when they discovered new information.

Beliefs often limit you and your view of the world around you. That is because your belief about yourself will turn out to be true— whether or not it is correct. If you change your beliefs, you change your world. But how can they be changed? Your beliefs are both formed and changed by the repetition of self-talk.

Beliefs and True Purpose

You bring your beliefs into harmony with your True Purpose by using positive self-talk to replace negative self-talk. Through this natural phenomenon that you have used all your life, you give new directions to your subconscious mind by talking to yourself in a different way, by giving more effective, more helpful and more positive information.

Changing negative beliefs is another step along the continuum of self-actualization, or toward embracing your True Purpose. Once you discover and start to live your True Purpose, an amazing thing happens: Your beliefs change to support you. Actually, it could not be otherwise, because to get to your True Purpose, it is necessary to address and work through each negative, non-supporting belief. This process requires that you analyze how these negative beliefs have stood in your way.

In her book, *Live Your Dream*, Joyce Chapman has a number of helpful exercises which have influenced the design of the exercises I have included here for you.

The following exercise, Beliefs That Prevent Me from Being the Type of Person I Want to Be, will help you look at some of your beliefs and will show you how they may have worked against you.

First, make a list of ten things you believe prevent you from being the type of person you want to be.

Then, record *how* each item prevents you from self-actualizing.

Next, explain *why* each belief works against you.

Finally, for each item, list the steps you can take to make each belief work for you. This part of the exercise may require that you modify, eliminate or redefine a belief.

Beliefs That Prevent Me from Being
the Type of Person I Want to Be

Beliefs That Prevent Me	How They Prevent Me	Why They Work to Prevent Me	Action to Make It Work for Me
1. I don't know how...	Sets up a mental block	Keeps you from trying	Learn how
2. I don't have what I need to get started	Closes the door to your trying	Makes you think you have an excuse	Improvise
3. I might fail...	Creates fear	Paralyzes desire	Trust your dreams
4. I can't afford it	Closes door to desire	Gives you an excuse	Take a second job
5. It's too hard...	Questions your skills	Enforces negative thoughts	Try it anyway
6.			
7.			
8.			
9.			
10			

Your Thoughts/Comments:

This exercise is designed to help you see how some of your beliefs work against you. Although the exercise is part of the process of discovering your True Purpose, merely looking at your beliefs and their effects on you is therapeutic. The more you repeat this exercise, the greater will be your benefits. That's why the 30-day True Purpose Journal[1] contains a daily exercise.

Structural Tension
Goal Setting and Visualization

Visualization is a little understood process, and many people dismiss it as either "pie in the sky" or mystical "bunk." Actually, it is firmly established in the principles of psychology. As part of the creative process, visualization uses perception to throw your system out of order so that you can create a new order of goal specific results. It is, in other words, the process of going from the old order to the new results.

This process of transfer between the old and the new creates a kind of tension between your current reality and your goals. Current reality is the present condition of your world as your perceive it. It is where you are now. Structural tension is created when your present reality differs from your goals or aspirations. It occurs when you realize that you are not where you want to be, or that you don't have what you want to have. Visualization both creates and helps resolve this tension.

Here is how visualization works: When you develop a vision or a goal, you create a contrast between your perception of your goal and current reality. This contrast creates structural tension. As a human being, you have a natural tendency to resolve tension and to restore order. So when you create this tension between your goal vision and your current reality, you naturally move to resolve that tension. You will resolve the tension in the direction of the strongest, most dominant perception—either your new goal or your current reality.

If you don't know how to make what you want the stronger, more dominant perception, you may find yourself stretching toward a goal only to be pulled back to current reality. When this happens, you will

---

[1]This journal may be purchased from the author. Address all inquiries to 4020 East Madison, Suite 200, Seattle, WA 98112.

tell yourself either that you've been sabotaged, or that you have changed goals, or that you really didn't want that goal in the first place.

This means that if you want to accomplish a goal, you must create a picture of the results that is stronger and more dominant than the picture of your current reality. To do this, you must adhere to two essential rules: 1) Define your current reality honestly, and 2) Make your goal the stronger, more dominant perception.

1. Define your current reality

You must define current reality the way it actually is. The structural tension that's created by the contrast between current reality and your goals depends on your assessing objectively where you are now.

2. Make your goal the stronger, more dominant perception.

You will create a strong, dominant goal perception only when you give great care and consideration to both your commitment and to the description of your goal. By commitment, I am referring to what Napoleon Hill called your burning desire. Without that burning desire, your goal will lack the emotional magnetism necessary to become stronger than and to dominate over your current reality. This domination of your goal over current reality is a natural result of living your True Purpose.

But commitment to a goal requires constant vigilance until the goal becomes so much a part of you that it is "seeded" in your subconscious. In order for this to happen, you must constantly and effectively reinforce your goals. An indispensable part of this reinforcement is through visualization of a sensory-rich goal vision. In Section 2, I will show you how to create a strong, dominant sensory-rich vision and how to envision it. Now I will show you the rules.

You remember that when you develop a goal, you create a contrast between your perception of your goal and current reality. In order to accomplish your goals, it is necessary for you to program your subconscious to accept your goals as being stronger and more dominant than your current reality. There are three simple rules for accomplishing this.

Rule 1: The more emotion you associate with a goal, the more strength it will have.

When you think of Jimmy Swaggart, what picture do you see? Probably his tearful confession of his—ah— "boyish curiosity." The tears streaming down his face probably left the same deep, powerful impression in your mind as it did mine. It does not matter how we felt about him; his actions were powerful. And that power came not from his words nor from his humility, it came from the emotions he attached to the moment. Those emotions captured our attention and made us notice. And it made us remember. In the same manner, you can give your goals strength and dominance over your current condition by attaching some strong emotions to them. You must feel something and feel it strongly.

I used this rule effectively in my own journey toward becoming an attorney. In 1973, after the scare of a bad grade, I started my visualization routine for the first time. Every morning when I awoke, I would immediately visualize what it would be like at my law school graduation. I would see my mother's face as I was handed my degree, and I would imagine the pride she felt. I would see the tears of joy streaming down her face. To this day, this picture stirs up within me strong and moving emotions. When I did graduate in 1975, the actual experience was almost exactly as I had visualized it.

When you build your vision, give it emotion. Paint into your picture of the vision those meanings which are dear to you. For instance, if it means a lot for you to start your own business, or get a degree, or change jobs, or get a promotion, attach those deep feelings of joy and satisfaction to your picture. If you add the emotions and apply the next two rules, you will soon find yourself moving toward your goal.

Rule 2: The more you repeat your goal, the stronger it will become.

Your subconscious mind accepts any information as true if you repeat it strongly and often enough. Advertisers have used this principle effectively for years. Tony Robbins illustrates this excellently when he asks us to complete the sentence, "Winston tastes good like a . . . ." We have heard that slogan repeated so many times that it is imbedded in our subconscious minds. I'm sure that you have already thought of many other advertising slogans that have become imbedded in your subconscious:

> "I'd walk a mile for a . . . . ."
> "Good to the very last . . . ."
> "Don't squeeze the . . . ."
> "Where's the . . . ."
> "I want to teach the world to sing in . . . ."

The point is when information is continuously repeated, your subconscious mind accepts it as true. So not only do you need to fill your goal with emotion, you must also repeat it often.

Rule 3: The more important the source, the stronger the goal.

Sources that are authoritative, influential or extraordinary tend to have the strongest impact on your acceptance of and reactions to a given goal. Not long ago, I spent some time with an outstanding, gifted organist. I met this 25-year-old organist just after he had given a breathtaking performance, and I asked him to share with me the secret of how he had mastered the organ so superbly. In so many words, he told me rule 3. He said that when he was 5 years old, a highly respected preacher had blessed his hands and told him God would use them to bring beautiful music into the world. From that moment on, he said, he would sit at the organ or piano in his church, remember what the preacher had told him, and start pounding on the keyboard. And then one day a tune began to emerge, and he has been playing ever since.

His story clearly illustrates the power of perceiving a goal as coming from an important source. You can use this principle to create your own strong, dominant goal perception. Make your self-talk more powerful by drawing on sources that you believe are important. A good way of doing this is to remind yourself of particular positive observations or statements that people have made to you, and remind yourself how many times they have said that particular thing. Or you can tell yourself about the similarities between your experiences and those of someone else who has already accomplished what you are trying to do.

I remember how I applied this technique during a particularly rough time in my life. I owned a small commuter airline and had put nearly all of my available funds in the company. I had spent a considerable amount of time pursuing a venture capital source, only to discover it was not interested in investing in the expansion of a small commuter airline. Then because of rising costs and other factors, I was forced to cease operating the airline even though it had just been awarded six international routes to Mexico.

On top of that, I was in a running battle with the IRS over a $130,000 tax lien. Then, in the middle of this battle, the bank that held a note secured by my home went into receivership and later fell into the hands of some people who engaged in what is, at best, questionable banking practices. The bank officers claimed, at first, that they had not received over $100,000 which had actually paid off the note, and they threatened foreclosure. When I presented the cancelled checks, they then gave me an accounting that applied all of the money to a personal installment note of $75,000 and to notes on two company cars. Then they proceeded with foreclosure. I had two lawyers try to stop the foreclosure, but they were not able to do so. Neither attorney did even a marginal job. The home in which my family and I had lived for 15 years was gone, and I was devastated. I could not believe what had happened.

Then I realized that to correct the wrong, I had to pick myself up and start again. I did this by reading about successful people who had experienced setbacks like mine. I developed a self-talk script in which I told myself that most people who reach great heights experience severe setbacks and even tragedies. I began to feel better and some amazing things started to happen.

Money started coming in from my business. My law practice earned more money in one year than I had earned in the previous five years, and those years had not been bad. All of a sudden, I realized that I was doing better than ever. Then those other negative conditions started to change. I terminated a negative business relationship, and hired two new lawyers, one to handle the bank problem and the other to handle the IRS.

Since then, in addition to wrongdoing in regard to my case, we have uncovered evidence of several unscrupulous activities by the bank, including forgery and inside trading. The bank has fired the attorney who instituted the foreclosure and is now suing her for malpractice for her failure to advise them that it was improper to apply funds in the manner they did and for other bad advice. Since then the bank officials have hinted at settlement.

My tax attorney has filed for a refund, and is now contesting the tax lien based on solid evidence that we don't owe the taxes. My life is full of joy and prosperity, and is relatively free of stress. But perhaps the greatest gift that came from all this is that I am now living my life dream of inspiring others to grow into themselves. I have been able to overcome these *battles* by programming a strong vision of my goal through the use of an authoritative source—others who had similar devastating experiences, but who went on to become highly successful.

Summary: Rule 1 + 2 + 3 = A Stronger, More Dominant Perception.

When you develop a rich goal vision filled with strong emotions and affirmations (see Section 4), and when you support that vision with authoritative or influential sources, and when you repeat the vision to yourself often through self-talk and visualization, you create the strongest dominant perception. This perception will then create structural tension that you will resolve in the direction of your goal vision.

The 3x3 daily workout found in the 30-day True Purpose Journal is designed to lead you through a daily self-talk exercise that includes all three of these rules for strengthening your perceptions of your goals. I have included a copy of this worksheet in this book. The worksheet is designed for you to use with your major goal. Please use a separate sheet, or set of sheets, for each goal. Here is how it works.

Section 1:	Write your Goal Statement. (Please read the instructions in Section 2, Chapter 3, Sensory-Rich Description, before you complete this part of the exercise.)
Section 2:	Write at least 25 affirmations about your goal. (Please read the instructions in Section 3, Chapter 3, Affirmations, before you complete this part of the exercise.)
Section 3:	Write your Sensory-Rich Goal Statement (Please read the instructions in Section 1, Chapter 3, True Goal Exercises, and Section 2, Chapter 3, Sensory-Rich Descriptions, before you complete this part of the exercise.)
	1. Look
	2. Sound
	3. Taste
	4. Touch
	5. Smell
	6. Emotions

If you need help in completing this form, follow the instructions in Section 2 of this book.

After you have completed the worksheet to your satisfaction, review it three times a day for three minutes each time.

Daily 3x3 Workout

Section One: My True Goal Is:

Section Two: My True Goal Affirmations Are:

1.

2.

3.

4.

5.

6.

7.

8.

9.

10.

11.

12.

13.

14.

15.

Daily 3x3 Workout

16.

17.

18.

19.

20.

21.

22.

23.

24.

25.

Section Three: My Sensory-Rich Goal Description Is:

Sight:

Sound:

Touch:

Smell:

Emotions:

Examples of Current Reality vs. Goals

When your perception of the difference between your current reality and your goals creates tension, you become uncomfortable, or even upset, and seek to resolve it. If your perception of your goal is not strong enough, you will bring your aspirations into line with your current reality.

That's what happened to Bob, a nurse who worked in the emergency room at a local hospital. He wanted to become a psychiatrist, so he set himself a goal and developed a vision of himself as a psychiatrist. But his vision was weak, vague, and lacked the quality of richness. Nevertheless, he held to his vision until his tension and frustration increased. This tension, of course, urged him to resolve it. But instead of resolving the tension toward his goal, Bob moved his aspiration backward toward his current reality of being a nurse in the emergency room. In doing this, he decided he didn't want to be a psychiatrist after all, but wanted to remain a nurse; and he changed his specialization to mental health. His decision lessened the tension, but the price he paid was that of little or no progress. The tension was resolved in favor of the stronger, more dominant goal perception. Bob's desire to become a psychiatrist simply was not strong enough to overcome his current reality.

Mary, an English major, had always secretly desired to fly jumbo jets. Mary's father was an airline pilot and many of their family friends were pilots. Mary, who had always been exposed to pilot talk around the dinner table, made frequent visits with her father to the cockpits of various types of planes. She knew a lot about aviation. When she firmly decided she wanted to become a pilot, she developed a sensory-rich vision, drawing upon her experiences and the information she had acquired about aviation.

The result was a strong, vivid sensory vision. She saw herself flying a jumbo jet; she heard herself talking on the radio; she could feel the instruments in her hands. She made all those things part of her vision. The longer she held this vision, the more the tension increased until she started moving toward becoming an airline pilot. She attended flight school and later got a job as a co-pilot. Today Mary is flying 747s.

Mary's and Bob's situations were structurally the same. They both had tension and they resolved it in the direction of the most dominant picture. The difference between Mary and Bob is that the strength and quality of Mary's vision drew her away from her current reality, while the vagueness and weakness of Bob's vision gave way to his current reality.

In the same manner, you repeat this process over and over again, in varying degrees, in your own life. When you fill your vision with as much vividness and aliveness as possible, you move yourself toward your vision. When your vision is weak, you lower your aspirations to bring them in line with your current reality.

Reticular Activating System

"If the only tool you have is a hammer, you tend to see every problem as a nail."   —A. Maslow

Creating your own future becomes easier when you use the reticular activating system (RAS). This system is a network of cells, located in the central cortex at the base of your brain, whose function is to determine your awareness. It filters in information you find valuable and screens out all other information. If you did not have this system, you would be bombarded by information and your life would be utter chaos and confusion.

To prevent this confusion, your reticular activating system narrows your field of consciousness. You develop a blind spot, called a scotoma, which prevents you from being conscious of those things that have no value to you until you give them value. For example, when you decide to buy a new car, you suddenly become conscious of the various types of cars on the street. Until then, you may not have noticed many of them. But once you decided you wanted one, your reticular activating system broadened your field of consciousness to let in information about cars. This system activates your awareness, moves some of it to your consciousness, and thereby determines your reality.

You determine your reality by your perception. What you perceive as true is basically the result of what you observe with your senses, and then what you tell yourself about what you observed. You will then act, or react, based upon what you have told yourself. If you were to see a crowd marching toward the end of town and tell yourself it was a parade, your reaction would be different than if you told yourself it was a rush to leave town. Your reticular activating system filters out information that does not confirm your *interpretation* of what you observe with your senses.

Once you set a goal, your reticular activating system activates your consciousness to ways of accomplishing that goal. If your goal is to buy a new car, then the comparison of different cars, the methods and the means of buying a car will come into your consciousness. Prior to establishing your goal, you may not have noticed any of these things. If your goal is to become a doctor, this system opens your consciousness to the opportunities and steps involved in becoming a doctor. Before you established that goal, you simply did not focus on them.

In creating what you want, you first establish a goal and then your reticular activating system opens your consciousness to opportunities and methods for realizing that goal. The goal always comes first, and then the method and opportunity to attain that goal follow. Visualization activates this system and establishes your goals.

Some people receive little positive input from the reticular activating system because they fill their minds with excuses—such as not having enough money, time, or other things. I know a gentleman whose passion was to become an artist and to create beauty through his talent for painting and sculpture. His excuse for not doing so was that he did not have enough training, nor did he have enough money to acquire any. He couldn't quit his job because without being adequately tested and trained, he wasn't sure whether he had what it took to be an artist. In his frustration, he talked to a friend who simply asked him, "What would you do if money and these other things were not a worry?" He said, "I would paint." That realization resulted in his changing careers and becoming an artist. Doors began to open for him. He saw opportunities where none existed before. His reticular activating system began to work for him. His paintings are well accepted, and he is living in the middle of his dream.

The moral of this story and the lesson of this topic is that you will see it when you believe it. The fact is that you already have the resources; they are waiting for you along the track of your life purpose.

Self-Efficacy

Your True Purpose is the door to the fullness and richness of life. "But," you may ask, "if I subconsciously know my True Purpose and if I am guided by it, why do I seem to attract such frustration and lack of fulfillment?" This question has to do with self-efficacy.

Efficacy is the ability to make things happen, the power to create and to produce the results that you desire. Self-efficacy is the sum of your self-appraisal:

- **Your self-esteem** (how you feel about yourself)
- **Your skills** (your tools and abilities)
- **Your resources** (your fund of knowledge, access to resources, motivation and the like)

Your own evaluation, or belief, about your ability to produce is what makes things happen. In short, self-efficacy is what you *think* you can do or be.

Studies have shown that people generally limit their desires to what they think they can have. For example, you won't allow yourself to desire a mansion if you think you don't deserve a mansion. You basically determine what you can have first and then you determine what you want. If you set a goal that is higher than your self-efficacy, you will eventually either lower your aspiration by abandoning the goal or raise your self-efficacy until your ability is even with your goal.

You can do more and better than you think. Your self-efficacy is always less than your true abilities. The problem is how do you raise your self-efficacy in order to reach a goal, especially if you don't believe you have the necessary skill, or worth, or resources? You can raise your self-efficacy by *believing* you have the ability to gather the resources, to acquire the skills, and to increase your worth. The exercises in this book all lead to greater self-efficacy.

Self-efficacy is directly related to how in touch you are with your True Purpose. The self-actualizing person is one of high efficacy; he is able to make things happen. He gathers resources and knows he is worthy of his goals. He moves toward his goals without evidence because he knows that they are attainable on his track of life. He knows that, like Joseph Campbell predicted, doors will open to his success that he did not even know existed.

Accountability

While self-efficacy is the ability to open doors and make things happen, accountability is taking the responsibility to do it. It means that you, and only you, are responsible for the quality of life you create for yourself. No one can impose anything on you without your consent. You make all the choices. Your present conditions are the results of your past choices. You chose to be obstructed or facilitated. You chose to be oppressed or freed. Nothing in your life escapes your choices. This does not mean you are responsible for things outside of your control, such as natural disasters and birth defects, but even in those things, you choose how you will respond.

You base your choices on your beliefs. Your beliefs are either positive and growth-oriented or negative and stifling. There are no neutral beliefs. Whether negative or positive, your reticular activating system filters out information that does not support your belief and lets in only that which does support it. So if you believe you are only an average person, student, housewife, father, mother, child or whatever, your reticular activating system will let in only what supports your belief.

The system works the same with your goals. Through a long line of your own choices, you eventually reach or miss your goals. Here's how it works: Your self-talk determines your beliefs; your beliefs determine your self-efficacy; your self-efficacy determines your aspirations; your aspirations determine your goals; your goals activate your reticular activating system; your reticular activating system removes your scotoma (blind spots) to opportunities; your opportunities determine your achievements and your achievements create your future.

Through what you tell yourself over and over (self-talk), you are ultimately responsible for the quality of life you create. Change your self-talk and you will change your beliefs. If your beliefs have led to negative results, you must change to positive self-talk. When that happens, your reticular activating system will supply information that supports your new positive belief. You will see opportunities when you believe you will succeed. You will see sources of money when you believe you should be prosperous. You will see products when you believe you should have a business. Your positive belief leads to a feeling of worthiness, and your self-efficacy rises. As you reach for your goal, your reticular activating system lets in information that shows you how to achieve it. You get ideas and then create results. Throughout all of this, you are in control. You are accountable for your future.

Accountability Exercise

The following exercise will help you internalize the concept of accountability.

In section one, list a condition or situation that you are unhappy about, that you judge as unwanted or negative. While conditions such as physical or mental handicaps or natural disasters are beyond your control, accountability allows you the freedom to make the best of them and, therefore, makes you responsible for what you do about them.

In section two, list five things that caused or in any way helped to create this negative condition. At this point don't be concerned about the source of these causes.

Under each cause statement of section three, you will identify ways in which you helped cause the condition and you will list steps you can take to correct it. Now do the exercise.

ACCOUNTABILITY EXERCISE

1. Condition or circumstances

_____

_____

_____

_____

2. Five causes of the condition or circumstances

   1. _____

   _____

   2. _____

   _____

   3. _____

   _____

   4. _____

   _____

   5. _____

   _____

3. For each cause, list how you contributed to the cause.

   Cause 1: _____

   _____

   Your Contribution: _____

   _____

   What could you have done to change or prevent the
   condition in section one? _____

   _____

   _____

   _____

What action can you take now to correct, eliminate, or improve the condition and to avoid its reoccurrence?

_____

_____

_____

_____

_____

Cause 2: _____

_____

Your Contribution: _____

_____

What could you have done to change or prevent the condition in section one? _____

_____

_____

_____

_____

What action can you take now to correct, eliminate, or improve that condition and to avoid its reoccurrence?

_____

_____

_____

_____

Cause 3: _____

_____

Your Contribution: _____

_____

What could you have done to change or prevent the
condition in section one? _____

_____

_____

_____

_____

What action can you take now to correct, eliminate, or
improve that condition and to avoid its reoccurrence?

_____

_____

_____

_____

_____

Cause 4: _____

_____

Your Contribution: _____

_____

What could you have done to change or prevent the
condition in section one? _____

_____

_____

_____

_____

What action can you take now to correct, eliminate, or
improve that condition and to avoid its reoccurrence?

_____

_____

_____

_____

_____

Cause 5: _____

_____

Your Contribution: _____

_____

What could you have done to change or prevent the
condition in section one? _____

_____

_____

_____

_____

What action can you take now to correct, eliminate, or
improve that condition and to avoid its reoccurrence?

_____

_____

_____

_____

Who had control over the creation of this condition? _____

_____

_____

_____

_____

_____

5. Your Comments: _____

_____

_____

_____

These exercises confront many situations in your life, and, consequently, require patience with yourself. But if you answer these questions carefully, with some deep thought and objectivity, you will be amazed at the tremendous sense of power you will experience from knowing that you control your own life.

Comfort Zone

Once you go through this period of adjustment, you will need to expand your comfort zone.

Some researchers for IBM did a study of salesmen who consistently made a certain level of sales. Some sold high volume and some low volume. IBM decided, as an experiment, to switch the territories of two groups of salesmen. So they put the salesmen who consistently had low sales in the high sales territory, and vice versa. They found that the salesmen who were originally in the high sales territory experienced high sales in the new territory, and the salesmen who had been in the low sales territory continued to experience low sales, even though they were in a territory that historically had been a high sales area. The researchers concluded that each person experiences an area of functionality that is called his comfort zone. When you expand beyond your comfort zone, you adjust your actions to bring yourself back into line with it. In day-to-day life, when you attempt to expand beyond your present situation, you will experience a tension and an uncomfortableness that tend to pull you back to your comfort zone.

An example of this would be a person who has never spoken before a large group, but who desires a career involving public speaking. When he experiences the uncomfortable feeling that public speaking creates, if there is not a stronger motivation, he will revert back to his old ways and give up the idea of public speaking.

The way to grow beyond your comfort zone is to give yourself a greater challenge and then grow toward it through the use of visualization, structural tension, higher self-efficacy and goal setting. As you use these methods, you will see your comfort zone increase.

Completion:
Clearing the Way

The biggest obstacles that stand between you and your True

Purpose are physical and mental blockages. These blockages are caused not by things that won't get out of your way, but by things that you have not moved out of the way. By moving things out of the way, you complete your involvement with them.

Completion is any action that results in the finalization of some incomplete goal, project, relationship, or situation you feel you should do something about. For example, you may have purchased several books a year ago that you still haven't read. This incomplete situation can clog your creative channels, slow your motivation, cloud your clarity, and stifle your growth. You can relieve these conditions by either reading the books or deciding not to read them. Either way, the project is complete. Whether you read them is not important, the important issue is to complete the transaction and move on.

I find myself completing situations quite often now. Some time ago, I had some disagreements with a fellow lawyer. Thoughts of those disagreements had lingered in my mind for quite a while and were, no doubt, negative and blocking influences. After I began to get in touch with my True Purpose, I found myself eliminating lingering situations that stood as obstacles. As a result, I wrote the following letter to this lawyer.

> I enjoyed talking with you in court a few days ago. Seeing you made me feel good. It also reminded me of something that I have been putting off doing—namely, telling you how much I admire you. You are probably wondering where all this is coming from. Well, I've been sober now for nearly a year. Sobriety forces me to recognize and acknowledge those people who deserve my praise and admiration. You are one of them. I have always admired and respected your courage to fight for what you believe in. Quietly, I always did root for you.

> Seeing you in court brought all these things back to mind and I decided to write you this letter. The feelings I have expressed here are really long overdue. I regret I was not a little more forthcoming about them in the past. I want to also take this opportunity to apologize for anything that I may have done that in any way obstructed or diminished our friendship.

> I look forward to talking with you soon. Let's have lunch.

> Yours truly,

> Phillip Aaron

The results of writing the letter were amazing. I felt like a load had been lifted from my back, and I began to see my purpose much clearer. I became convinced that clearing out incomplete situations—whether physical, mental, emotional—is an indispensable part of connecting with my True Purpose.

The more you complete old, stale situations, the more energy, clarity and focus you have. You become more in touch with yourself, your outlook becomes fresher and more positive, and your ability to see solutions becomes stronger. Initially, this clearing up process precedes living your True Purpose and, indeed, helps lead to the discovery of your True Purpose. Later, however, when you start living your True Purpose, you will find yourself completing all the time.

I dislike most of the day-to-day practice of law. So after committing to my True Purpose, I decided to gradually move out of law into the field of my True Purpose, and I set up a timetable for moving into my passion of inspiring others to be the best that they can be. This act of clearing out emotional blocks created more openness in me and cleared a path for a closeness to and a realization of my purpose in life.

Many blocks and incompletions stand in the way of your fully connecting with your True Purpose. These obstacles can be as simple and as mundane as clearing out your closet, or cleaning your house and moving things out of the way, or as critical as dealing with a painful relationship. Whatever you perceive as being incomplete stands in the way of your feeling open to and connected with your True Purpose. Those things should be cleared out. This does not mean that you have to throw things away, terminate relationships or anything of that nature (although you may do that). It may mean that you simply have to accept the fact that the situations are there and do something to finalize and clear them out.

In the completion exercise that follows, make a list of at least two things that you feel are unresolved or incomplete in each of the following categories: personal, social, physical, emotional, home, business, and career. When I did my list in that way, one of the top items was a business relationship with some partners in another city. From my perspective, this relationship was not beneficial or productive. I had stayed in the relationship, hoping that somehow it would get better but it had not. After doing this exercise myself, I realized that to improve the relationship I had to resolve and complete it in one way or another. After giving it sufficient thought, I decided that the best way was to terminate the relationship. As a result, I sold my interest in the business to the remaining partners. The act of selling was such a powerful release for me that I found myself propelled further along the road of living my purpose and mission in life. I discovered that the resentment and anger I had harbored toward my partners had prevented me from seeing opportunities, from building a good relationship with them, and from fully presenting myself to others in a positive way.

You may have a similar blockage that needs to be cleared up in some fashion. The following exercise will help you bring some of these things to mind and deal with them.

For each item you list in this exercise, indicate what you will do to complete it and when you will do it. I suggest that you complete one item per day for the next thirty days. When you have done this, you will be truly amazed at how you feel. Even in the first two weeks you will feel clearer, more focused and more energetic. In thirty days, you'll be ecstatic with yourself. Also one item per day is not too exhausting. Many of your incomplete situations can be handled by a phone call, a letter or a brief conversation. With some things you may only be able to start the completion process—for example, reading a book. In such cases, the situation is considered complete when you make the commitment and follow through on the action. Every day look at your completion project; you will find the reminder helpful.

Completion Exercise

List two incomplete situations in each of the following areas:

Personal (attitude, nurturing goals, self-improvement, romance, etc.)

1.

2.

Physical (health, dress, exercise, etc.)

1.

2.

Emotional (anger, hurt, resentment, jealousy, etc.)

1.

2.

Home Environment (cleaning, remodeling, changing, acquiring, etc.)

1.

2.

Business (starting, improving, hiring, firing, etc.)

1.

2.

Careers (selecting, changing, preparing, etc.)

1.

2.

Clearing the Way

The aim of completion is to clear the way for you to create the quality of life you want. Clearing the way is essential to reaching and embracing your True Purpose, or, as Maslow would say, self-actualization. Clearing the way helps you find out who you are, where you are, what you genuinely like and dislike, what is good or bad for you, and where you are going. It opens you up to yourself. The process has nothing to do with blame; its only objective is to heal and to open. Clearing the way is like the lyrics of a blues song called "Blues Will Never Die" which says,

> The blues don't ask you where you are going, and the blues don't care where you've been.

It is only important that you don't stay where you've been and that you move to where you want to go in your life.

Clearing the way involves identifying things that stand between you and what you want. It involves seeing those things in two ways:

- First, for what they are or for what you really believe about them.
- Second, for how your beliefs support them, thereby perpetuating your blockage.

The following exercises are all designed to help you accomplish both objectives. They include:

- I am honest when... because...
- I am least honest when... because...
- I deserve... because...
- I don't deserve... because...
- What I believe about my ability is...
- The thing in my past that aids me now is... because it helps me to...
- The thing in my past that hinders me now is... because...
- What I believe about my past is...
- What I believe about my future is...
- What I really want is...
- What stands between me and what I really want is...
- I feel happiest when I... because...
- I feel least happy when I...because...
- I like myself most when I...because...

- I like myself least when I...because...
- Who am I? I am...

These exercises are designed to lead to a greater consciousness rather than to any specific conclusion. They will help you discard false and limiting beliefs. Merely knowing and recognizing your false and limiting beliefs will free you, provided you truly recognize them as such. That's why it is important that you take some time, after each exercise, to write in your journal any thoughts or feelings you have about the exercise. You should review your notes every day as part of your improvement program.

These exercises are intended to elicit the free flow of information and are intentionally loosely structured to allow you to answer in a manner most suitable for you.

You may find that some of the exercises will bring forth the same or similar responses. This is because, when you do these exercises, you are addressing some recurring fundamental issues. For example, suppose that you find that you distrust yourself and that this distrust is one of the things you like least about yourself. If you feel that you do not deserve what you want, this distrust could be the reason. So don't be surprised when you find similar responses to some of the sentence completion exercises; instead, look to see if they are in some way interconnected.

In addition to the written exercises, do at least one of the clearing the way exercises each day for thirty days while sitting or standing in front of a mirror, looking into your eyes and completing the sentences aloud. Record your responses with a tape recorder, and play them back as a part of your review.

After you have done the exercises, you are ready to start exploring your True Purpose and learning how to actualize it by using your talents to reach your goals.

Congratulations! You have come a long way.

Clearing the Way Exercises
I am honest when... because...

Complete each of the following twenty sentences.

1. I am honest when...

    because...

2. I am honest when...

    because...

3. I am honest when...

    because...

4. I am honest when...

    because...

5. I am honest when...

    because...

6. I am honest when...

   because...

7. I am honest when...

   because...

8. I am honest when...

   because...

9. I am honest when...

   because...

10. I am honest when...

    because...

11. I am honest when...

    because...

12. I am honest when...

    because...

13. I am honest when...

    because...

14. I am honest when...

    because...

15. I am honest when...

    because...

16. I am honest when . . .

because . . .

17. I am honest when . . .

because . . .

18. I am honest when . . .

because . . .

19. I am honest when . . .

because . . .

20. I am honest when . . .

because . . .

Write down your thoughts about your answers. Is your belief valid? Has it served you? What patterns do you see? What changes, if any, do you want to make?

I am least honest when... because...

Complete each of the following twenty sentences.

1.   I am least honest when...

     because...

2.   I am least honest when...

     because...

3.   I am least honest when...

     because...

4.   I am least honest when...

     because...

5.   I am least honest when...

     because...

6. I am least honest when...

    because...

7. I am least honest when...

    because...

8. I am least honest when...

    because...

9. I am least honest when...

    because...

10. I am least honest when...

    because...

11. I am least honest when...

   because...

12. I am least honest when...

   because...

13. I am least honest when...

   because...

14. I am least honest when...

   because...

15. I am least honest when...

   because...

16. I am least honest when...

    because...

17. I am least honest when...

    because...

18. I am least honest when...

    because...

19. I am least honest when...

    because...

20. I am least honest when...

    because...

Write down your thoughts about your answers. Is your belief valid? Has it served you? What patterns do you see? What changes, if any, do you want to make?

I deserve... because...

Complete each of the following twenty sentences.

1.   I deserve...

     because...

2.   I deserve...

     because...

3.   I deserve...

     because...

4.   I deserve...

     because...

5.   I deserve...

     because...

6.   I deserve...

     because...

7.   I deserve...

     because...

8.   I deserve...

     because...

9.   I deserve...

     because...

10. I deserve...

     because...

11. I deserve...

     because...

12. I deserve...

     because...

13. I deserve...

     because...

14. I deserve...

     because...

15. I deserve...

     because...

16. I deserve...

     because...

17. I deserve...

     because...

18. I deserve...

     because...

19. I deserve...

     because...

20. I deserve...

     because...

Write down your thoughts about your answers. Is your belief valid? Has it served you? What patterns do you see? What changes, if any, do you want to make?

I don't deserve... because...

Complete each of the following twenty sentences.

1.   I don't deserve...

     because...

2.   I don't deserve...

     because...

3.   I don't deserve...

     because...

4.   I don't deserve...

     because...

5.   I don't deserve...

     because...

6. I don't deserve...

    because...

7. I don't deserve...

    because...

8. I don't deserve...

    because...

9. I don't deserve...

    because...

10. I don't deserve...

    because...

11.   I don't deserve...

because...

12.   I don't deserve...

because...

13.   I don't deserve...

because...

14.   I don't deserve...

because...

15.   I don't deserve...

because...

16. I don't deserve...

    because...

17. I don't deserve...

    because...

18. I don't deserve...

    because...

19. I don't deserve...

    because...

20. I don't deserve...

    because...

Write down your thoughts about your answers. Is your belief valid?
Has it served you? What patterns do you see? What changes, if any,
do you want to make?

What I believe about my ability is...

Complete each of the following twenty sentences.

1.   What I believe about my ability is...

2.   What I believe about my ability is...

3.   What I believe about my ability is...

4.   What I believe about my ability is...

5.   What I believe about my ability is...

6.   What I believe about my ability is...

7.   What I believe about my ability is...

8.   What I believe about my ability is...

9.   What I believe about my ability is...

10. What I believe about my ability is...

11.   What I believe about my ability is. . .

12.   What I believe about my ability is. . .

13.   What I believe about my ability is. . .

14.   What I believe about my ability is. . .

15.   What I believe about my ability is. . .

16.   What I believe about my ability is. . .

17.   What I believe about my ability is. . .

18.   What I believe about my ability is. . .

19.   What I believe about my ability is. . .

20.   What I believe about my ability is. . .

Write down your thoughts about your answers. Is your belief valid? Has it served you? What patterns do you see? What changes, if any, do you want to make?

The thing in my past that aids me now is...
because it helps me to...

Complete each of the following twenty sentences.

1.   The thing in my past that aids me now is...

       because it helps me to...

2.   The thing in my past that aids me now is...

       because it helps me to...

3.   The thing in my past that aids me now is...

       because it helps me to...

4.   The thing in my past that aids me now is...

       because it helps me to...

5.   The thing in my past that aids me now is...

       because it helps me to...

6.   The thing in my past that aids me now is...

     because it helps me to...

7.   The thing in my past that aids me now is...

     because it helps me to...

8.   The thing in my past that aids me now is...

     because it helps me to...

9.   The thing in my past that aids me now is...

     because it helps me to...

10. The thing in my past that aids me now is...

     because it helps me to...

11.   The thing in my past that aids me now is...

      because it helps me to...

12.   The thing in my past that aids me now is...

      because it helps me to...

13.   The thing in my past that aids me now is...

      because it helps me to...

14.   The thing in my past that aids me now is...

      because it helps me to...

15.   The thing in my past that aids me now is...

      because it helps me to...

16. The thing in my past that aids me now is...

    because it helps me to...

17. The thing in my past that aids me now is...

    because it helps me to...

18. The thing in my past that aids me now is...

    because it helps me to...

19. The thing in my past that aids me now is...

    because it helps me to...

20. The thing in my past that aids me now is...

    because it helps me to...

Write down your thoughts about your answers. Is your belief valid? Has it served you? What patterns do you see? What changes, if any, do you want to make?

The thing in my past that hinders me now is...
It hinders me because...

Complete each of the following twenty sentences.

1. The thing in my past that hinders me now is...

    It hinders me because...

2. The thing in my past that hinders me now is...

    It hinders me because...

3. The thing in my past that hinders me now is...

    It hinders me because...

4. The thing in my past that hinders me now is...

    It hinders me because...

5. The thing in my past that hinders me now is...

    It hinders me because...

6. The thing in my past that hinders me now is...

   It hinders me because...

7. The thing in my past that hinders me now is...

   It hinders me because...

8. The thing in my past that hinders me now is...

   It hinders me because...

9. The thing in my past that hinders me now is...

   It hinders me because...

10. The thing in my past that hinders me now is...

    It hinders me because...

11. The thing in my past that hinders me now is...

It hinders me because...

12. The thing in my past that hinders me now is...

It hinders me because...

13. The thing in my past that hinders me now is...

It hinders me because...

14. The thing in my past that hinders me now is...

It hinders me because...

15. The thing in my past that hinders me now is...

It hinders me because...

16.   The thing in my past that hinders me now is...

It hinders me because...

17.   The thing in my past that hinders me now is...

It hinders me because...

18.   The thing in my past that hinders me now is...

It hinders me because...

19.   The thing in my past that hinders me now is...

It hinders me because...

20.   The thing in my past that hinders me now is...

It hinders me because...

Write down your thoughts about your answers. Is your belief valid? Has it served you? What patterns do you see? What changes, if any, do you want to make?

What I believe about my past is...

Complete each of the following twenty sentences.

1.   What I believe about my past is...

2.   What I believe about my past is...

3.   What I believe about my past is...

4.   What I believe about my past is...

5.   What I believe about my past is...

6.   What I believe about my past is...

7.   What I believe about my past is...

8.   What I believe about my past is...

9.   What I believe about my past is...

10. What I believe about my past is...

11. What I believe about my past is. . .

12. What I believe about my past is. . .

13. What I believe about my past is. . .

14. What I believe about my past is. . .

15. What I believe about my past is. . .

16. What I believe about my past is. . .

17. What I believe about my past is. . .

18. What I believe about my past is. . .

19. What I believe about my past is. . .

20. What I believe about my past is. . .

Write down your thoughts about your answers. Is your belief valid?
Has it served you? What patterns do you see? What changes, if any,
do you want to make?

What I believe about my future is. . .

Complete each of the following twenty sentences.

1.   What I believe about my future is. . .

2.   What I believe about my future is. . .

3.   What I believe about my future is. . .

4.   What I believe about my future is. . .

5.   What I believe about my future is. . .

6.   What I believe about my future is. . .

7.   What I believe about my future is. . .

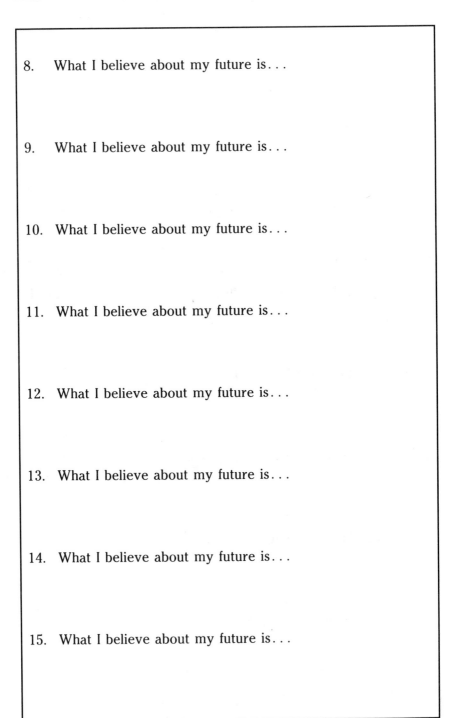

8. What I believe about my future is...

9. What I believe about my future is...

10. What I believe about my future is...

11. What I believe about my future is...

12. What I believe about my future is...

13. What I believe about my future is...

14. What I believe about my future is...

15. What I believe about my future is...

16. What I believe about my future is...

17. What I believe about my future is...

18. What I believe about my future is...

19. What I believe about my future is...

20. What I believe about my future is...

Write down your thoughts about your answers. Is your belief valid? Has it served you? What patterns do you see? What changes, if any, do you want to make?

What I really want is...

Complete each of the following twenty sentences.

1. What I really want is...

2. What I really want is...

3. What I really want is...

4. What I really want is...

5. What I really want is...

6. What I really want is...

7. What I really want is...

8. What I really want is...

9. What I really want is...

10. What I really want is...

11.   What I really want is...

12.   What I really want is...

13.   What I really want is...

14.   What I really want is...

15.   What I really want is...

16.   What I really want is...

17.   What I really want is...

18.   What I really want is...

19.   What I really want is...

20.   What I really want is...

Write down your thoughts about your answers. Is your belief valid? Has it served you? What patterns do you see? What changes, if any, do you want to make?

What stands between me and
what I really want is...

Complete each of the following twenty sentences.

1.   What stands between me and what I really want is...

2.   What stands between me and what I really want is...

3.   What stands between me and what I really want is...

4.   What stands between me and what I really want is...

5.   What stands between me and what I really want is...

6.   What stands between me and what I really want is...

7.   What stands between me and what I really want is...

8. What stands between me and what I really want is. . .

9. What stands between me and what I really want is. . .

10. What stands between me and what I really want is. . .

11. What stands between me and what I really want is. . .

12. What stands between me and what I really want is. . .

13. What stands between me and what I really want is. . .

14. What stands between me and what I really want is. . .

15. What stands between me and what I really want is. . .

16.   What stands between me and what I really want is...

17.   What stands between me and what I really want is...

18.   What stands between me and what I really want is...

19.   What stands between me and what I really want is...

20.   What stands between me and what I really want is...

Write down your thoughts about your answers. Is your belief valid? Has it served you? What patterns do you see? What changes, if any, do you want to make?

I feel happiest when I...because...

Complete each of the following twenty sentences.

1. I feel happiest when I...

    because...

2. I feel happiest when I...

    because...

3. I feel happiest when I...

    because...

4. I feel happiest when I...

    because...

5. I feel happiest when I...

    because...

6.   I feel happiest when I...

     because...

7.   I feel happiest when I...

     because...

8.   I feel happiest when I...

     because...

9.   I feel happiest when I...

     because...

10. I feel happiest when I...

     because...

11. I feel happiest when I...

because...

12. I feel happiest when I...

because...

13. I feel happiest when I...

because...

14. I feel happiest when I...

because...

15. I feel happiest when I...

because...

16. I feel happiest when I...

    because...

17. I feel happiest when I...

    because...

18. I feel happiest when I...

    because...

19. I feel happiest when I...

    because...

20. I feel happiest when I...

    because...

Write down your thoughts about your answers. Is your belief valid? Has it served you? What patterns do you see? What changes, if any, do you want to make?

I feel least happy when I. . .because. . .

Complete each of the following twenty sentences.

1. I feel least happy when I. . .

   because. . .

2. I feel least happy when I. . .

   because. . .

3. I feel least happy when I. . .

   because. . .

4. I feel least happy when I. . .

   because. . .

5. I feel least happy when I. . .

   because. . .

6.   I feel least happy when I. . .

     because. . .

7.   I feel least happy when I. . .

     because. . .

8.   I feel least happy when I. . .

     because. . .

9.   I feel least happy when I. . .

     because. . .

10.   I feel least happy when I. . .

      because. . .

11. I feel least happy when I...

    because...

12. I feel least happy when I...

    because...

13. I feel least happy when I...

    because...

14. I feel least happy when I...

    because...

15. I feel least happy when I...

    because...

16. I feel least happy when I...

because...

17. I feel least happy when I...

because...

18. I feel least happy when I...

because...

19. I feel least happy when I...

because...

20. I feel least happy when I...

because...

Write down your thoughts about your answers. Is your belief valid? Has it served you? What patterns do you see? What changes, if any, do you want to make?

I like myself most when I . . . because . . .

Complete each of the following twenty sentences.

1.   I like myself most when I . . .

      because . . .

2.   I like myself most when I . . .

      because . . .

3.   I like myself most when I . . .

      because . . .

4.   I like myself most when I . . .

      because . . .

5.   I like myself most when I . . .

      because . . .

6. I like myself most when I. . .

    because. . .

7. I like myself most when I. . .

    because. . .

8. I like myself most when I. . .

    because. . .

9. I like myself most when I. . .

    because. . .

10. I like myself most when I. . .

    because. . .

11. I like myself most when I...

because...

12. I like myself most when I...

because...

13. I like myself most when I...

because...

14. I like myself most when I...

because...

15. I like myself most when I...

because...

16. I like myself most when I . . .

   because . . .

17. I like myself most when I . . .

   because . . .

18. I like myself most when I . . .

   because . . .

19. I like myself most when I . . .

   because . . .

20. I like myself most when I . . .

   because . . .

Write down your thoughts about your answers. Is your belief valid? Has it served you? What patterns do you see? What changes, if any, do you want to make?

I like myself least when I . . . because . . .

Complete each of the following twenty sentences.

1.   I like myself least when I . . .

   because . . .

2.   I like myself least when I . . .

   because . . .

3.   I like myself least when I . . .

   because . . .

4.   I like myself least when I . . .

   because . . .

5.   I like myself least when I . . .

   because . . .

6.   I like myself least when I...

because...

7.   I like myself least when I...

because...

8.   I like myself least when I...

because...

9.   I like myself least when I...

because...

10. I like myself least when I...

because...

11. I like myself least when I...

because...

12. I like myself least when I...

because...

13. I like myself least when I...

because...

14. I like myself least when I...

because...

15. I like myself least when I...

because...

16.   I like myself least when I...

because...

17.   I like myself least when I...

because...

18.   I like myself least when I...

because...

19.   I like myself least when I...

because...

20.   I like myself least when I...

because...

Write down your thoughts about your answers. Is your belief valid? Has it served you? What patterns do you see? What changes, if any, do you want to make?

Who am I? I am...

Complete each of the following twenty sentences.

1. Who am I? I am...

2. Who am I? I am...

3. Who am I? I am...

4. Who am I? I am...

5. Who am I? I am...

6. Who am I? I am...

7. Who am I? I am...

8.　Who am I? I am...

9.　Who am I? I am...

10.　Who am I? I am...

11.　Who am I? I am...

12.　Who am I? I am...

13.　Who am I? I am...

14.　Who am I? I am...

15.　Who am I? I am...

16.   Who am I? I am...

17.   Who am I? I am...

18.   Who am I? I am...

19.   Who am I? I am...

20.   Who am I? I am...

Write down your thoughts about your answers. Is your belief valid? Has it served you? What patterns do you see? What changes, if any, do you want to make?

What Is This Inner Power
and How Do We Tap It?

You have the ability to accomplish great things and to make great contributions to the world. You have within you the ability to do something expertly. But, perhaps, like most people, you have gone through life not focused on what you really want and not accomplishing much. You may even have observed that a few people seem to attract success, prosperity and happiness almost effortlessly. It is as though they were caught up in a flow that carries them from one proper port to the next. You may have looked at these people and asked, "How is it that things come to them so easily and naturally?" Perhaps you attributed their success to luck, a charmed life, or some other vague term.

What is it that allows one person to achieve success, while another person of equal ability and knowledge constantly experiences the lack of success? I believe the only difference between the two is that one has tapped his inner power, while the other has not. Or to state it differently, one has discovered and committed to his True Purpose, True Talent and True Goal, while the other has not.

People who accomplish great things commit their lives to their True Purpose and use their True Talents to pursue their True Goals. They often must overcome tremendous odds, yet they emerge victorious. If you were to study their lives, you would see a fairly consistent pattern running through them. They all seem to have developed a force within which makes them unstoppable. This conquering force emerges from their commitment to purpose and their persistence. Abraham Lincoln had this conquering force; even though he failed time and time again, he persistently tried again until eventually he won.

BIOGRAPHICAL OUTLINE

Abraham Lincoln

1. Failed at business at 21.

2. Lost in a legislative race at age 22.

3. Failed again in business at 24.

4. Overcame the death of his sweetheart at 26.

5. Had a nervous breakdown at age 27.

6. Lost a congressional race at age 34.

7. Lost a congressional race at age 36.

8. Lost a senatorial race at age 45.

9. Failed in an effort to become vice-president at age 47.

10. Lost a senatorial race at age 49.

11. Elected president of the United States at age 52.

During this section, you will be asked to participate in exercises designed to lead you to the discovery of your True Purpose. From your True Purpose, you will go on to discover both your True Talent and your True Goal. Now bear in mind that you may have several talents and several goals, but it is important to identify your paramount talent and goal and to bring them into harmony so that you can create the life that you want to create.

In the following exercise, a series of questions will help you identify the significance and impact of a person's True Purpose, True Talent and True Goal on his achievements. Select a person whom you know well enough to answer the following questions about. You may choose someone you know personally, or someone you've read about extensively, or someone whose career in television or motion pictures you've followed.

PROFILE OF A SUCCESSFUL PERSON

Name: _____

In the space above, write the name of a successful person other than yourself. This may be someone you know or have read about who is successful by your standards. Then answer the following questions about that person.

1. What is this person's purpose in life?

2. What is this person's paramount talent?

3. What is this person's paramount goal?

4. How does the person use his paramount talent to accomplish his goal and purpose in life?

   a. How does he use his talent to accomplish his purpose?

   b. How does he use his talent to accomplish his goal?

5. What did you look at to determine the person's True Purpose?

6. What attitudes and beliefs did you observe this person living by?

7. List this person's habits. Select from among these the habits you would like to possess and develop.

It is logical to assume that a person's activities and focus will align with his True Purpose or mission in life. You should have been able, therefore, to identify this person's life purpose from his attitudes, commitments and activities.

Look again at the profile you did on the successful person.

1. What rule or principle can you deduce from your answers to the questions?

2. What do you think the results would have been if this person's True Purpose was either ill-defined or completely different from his activities?

A pattern among high achievers seems to suggest that True Purpose is the foundation of all their actions, beliefs and accomplishments. They seem to focus consistently on their True Purpose, and this focus flows through to their specific goals and talents. They project an image of consistency, direction and certainty. Their personalities are attractive to us because all of these things add up to credibility. We trust them.

High achievers provide a clear example of how life works for those who find and pursue their True Purpose. It works because they are living the life they ought to be living, and therefore they are doing what they ought to be doing. Success for them is a natural process. You can experience this same process and it will lead to your success. All that is required is that you identify and commit yourself to living your True Purpose.

Identifying Your True Purpose

The first step in pursuing and identifying your own True Purpose is answering three questions about yourself.

1. Do you feel you are on this planet for a purpose?

2. Do you feel you have a purpose in this life?

3. Do you know what that purpose is?

Now, think about your answers while I make a couple of observations. Most of us feel that we have a purpose in life, but, at the same time, we do not know what that purpose is. The conflict between having a purpose and not knowing what it is causes frustration, unhappiness and lack of success. We all want to be successful; we all want to be happy. We even know that being successful and happy means living the kind of life we ought to be living, yet most of us don't know what kind of life that actually is.

But do we spend time on a consistent basis—daily, weekly, monthly—searching for our True Purpose? Probably less than one percent of the population does. We spend our time trying to find happiness and success, but we spend little time trying to discover our True Purpose. That is like trying to drink from a cup without turning it up to your lips. It is impossible. You cannot find happiness, success, or fulfillment without first discovering and committing fully to your True Purpose in life. You see, your True Purpose is a steam that will carry you from where you are to where you ought to be. Some of us are in that stream, but most of us are not. Unfortunately, you cannot enter the stream, or even find it, by starting with the vague concept of finding success or happiness. You can only enter it from its beginning, and the beginning is in discovering and committing to your True Purpose. So let's begin your journey toward success and happiness by discovering your True Purpose.

What Is True Purpose?

Joseph Campbell, the philosopher and author, who died on October 31, 1987, was the world's foremost authority on mythology, which he defines as those basic beliefs that make up our attitudes and cultural biases. Campbell made a profound and clear definition of True Purpose in an interview with Bill Moyers on the PBS series, *The Power of Myth*. Campbell used the word "bliss" to describe what I call your True Purpose.

Moyers asked Campbell, "What happens when you follow your bliss?"

"You come to bliss," Campbell said. "In the Middle Ages, a favorite image that occurs in many, many contexts is the wheel of fortune. There's the hub of the wheel, and there is the revolving rim of the wheel. For example, if you are attached to the rim of the wheel of fortune, you will be either above going down or at the bottom coming up. *But if you are at the hub, you are in the same place all the time.* That is the sense of the marriage vow—I take you in health or sickness, in wealth or poverty: going up or going down. But I take you as my center, and you are my bliss, not the wealth that you might bring me, not the social prestige, but you. That is following your bliss."

"Do you ever have this sense when you are following your bliss, as I have at moments, of being helped by hidden hands?" Moyers asked.

"All the time," Campbell responded. "It is miraculous. I even have a superstition that has grown on me as the result of invisible hands coming all the time—namely, that if you do follow your bliss you put yourself on a kind of track that has been there all the while, waiting for you, and the life that you ought to be living is the one that you are living. When you can see that, you begin to meet people who are in the field of your bliss, and they open the doors to you. I say, follow your bliss and don't be afraid, and doors will open where you didn't know they were going to be. Wherever you are—if you are following your bliss, you are enjoying that refreshment, that life within you, all the time."

The bliss that Campbell referred to is what I call your True Purpose. It is that self-discovery and self-awareness that puts you on your invisible track in life, that leads you to live the life you ought to be living. It is your mission in life. It is that driving force that enables you to accomplish great things; it is your foundation; it is the center place from which everything that is proper and appropriate for you grows.

What does following your True Purpose mean?

Following your True Purpose is being true to yourself, which means having the courage to be an individual, the courage to stand alone sometimes, and the courage to follow your heart.

All the responses and benefits you get come as a result of others acknowledging that you are true to yourself. When you are true to yourself, you are operating on a basic human level that everyone can understand: You have penetrated and gone beyond all barriers to become yourself. There seems to be some sort of connection that you have with other people when you are true to yourself. That's why the world responds to a Lech Walesa, a Nelson Mandela, a John F. Kennedy and a Martin Luther King, Jr.—they are, or were, true to themselves.

Lech Walesa was an electrician in the shipyards who believed that the workers of Poland were not being treated fairly, so he started doing something about it. Through the unions, he fought long and hard to gain workers' rights, stressing that the gain must be accomplished without violence. In 1980, he became the head of the labor movement, called Solidarity, which was composed of some 50 Polish trade unions. In November of that year, the Polish government recognized Solidarity; it was the first time any labor organization outside of the Communist Party had been recognized. In December 1981, the government established martial law and banned Solidarity, sending Walesa and many others to prison. After a year, Walesa was released and he continued to work for workers' rights. In 1989, the ban was lifted and elections were allowed for Parliament. Almost every candidate Walesa and Solidarity supported were elected.

People are also attracted to you when you are true to yourself. Some won't agree with you or with what you are doing, but many will. They all will respect you, however, when you are truly committed, open, honest and true to yourself. All you have to do to see that this is true is to ask yourself these questions:

1. Do I prefer to deal with a person who is genuine or with one who is phoney?
2. Which person deserves respect for his convictions?

Obviously, you would prefer to deal with a person who is genuine, and you respect a person who lives by his convictions, even if you do not agree with him.

How do you know when you are living your True Purpose?

When you are living your True purpose, life becomes relatively easy. The line between work and play blurs, and every decision you make is based upon whether it supports your True Purpose. You have a sense of destiny, of direction, and of self-confidence. You know what you want, you know where you want to go, and you allow your inner voice to lead you there. Your confidence and your sureness go beyond the arrogance of ego to what others may mistakenly believe to be humility, when, in fact, it is effortless living that stems from knowing that no one and nothing can stop you or take you away from your life purpose.

At first glance, this statement seems to be more hype than substance; however, closer scrutiny reveals its profound truth. As I said earlier, life is made up of choices. We choose to be happy or unhappy; we choose mediocrity or excellence. Much of our lives' difficulties stems from our uncertainty about what choices we should make and from our fear of making the wrong choices. When you are living your True Purpose, the choices become easy to make. For every decision you make is based upon whether it will support your True Purpose. This clarity heightens your self-esteem and gives a sense of destiny and true confidence.

You begin to accomplish goals that are within your True Purpose in a manner that is easy and enjoyable. Your personality becomes so focused on your life purpose that you take on the characteristic commonly called charisma. Creativity becomes second nature to you for it flows from your core. These results, on the one hand, are remarkable and may even seem miraculous, while, on the other hand, they are comfortable and natural. They are a part of you.

We have seen this characteristic in many historical figures. Mozart, for example, wrote symphonies as though they were being dictated to him by some mysterious force. Taylor Caldwell, the popular American author, often writes late into the night and seldom has to re-write her manuscripts. I am sure you can think of many other examples. The point is that once you commit to your life purpose, you place yourself into the stream of bliss, and you receive the aid of those "invisible hands" that Joseph Campbell mentioned.

I'm sure that you, like all of us, have had those fleeting moments and flashes of profound insight and excellence that come from momentary attachments to your life purpose. Maslow called these peak performance experiences. In *Motivation and Personality,* he says that in these experiences there are "feelings of limitless horizons opening up to the vision, the feeling of being simultaneously more powerful and also more helpless than one ever was before, the feeling of great ecstasy and wonder and awe, the loss of placing in time and space with, finally, the conviction that something extremely important and valuable had happened." He says that these experiences to some extent transform and strengthen the person even in daily life.

Maslow says that in peak experiences there is a "tremendous intensification of any of the experiences in which there is loss of self or transcendence of it, such as problem centering, intense concentration, intense sensuous experience, or self-forgetful and intense enjoyment of music or art."

These flashes of insight are just little examples to let you know your purpose is there and that it represents a call from within for you to come and embrace it. Those were passing moments only because you have not reached down into your essence to connect with and commit to your purpose.

Joseph Campbell described the individual who doesn't commit to his True Purpose as one on whom he has great pity. He said, "Yes, he is the one who evokes compassion, the poor chap. To see him stumbling around when all the waters of life are right there really evokes one's pity."

Now we all know many people who are stumbling around, ignoring life's waters that are right inside them. They are the ones who are insecure, who lack focus, who feel like they have not found themselves, who lack self-esteem, and who allow themselves to spend time on unproductive emotions such as anger, resentment and the like. They are the ones who keep almost making it, the ones who could have, but didn't. They are the ones who resent the progress of others.

Sound familiar? This list probably hits all of us somewhere.

- Feels insecure
- Lacks focus
- Has not found self
- Has low self-esteem
- Displays anger
- Nurses resentment
- Almost makes it
- Could have but. . .

Should some of these descriptions fit you, that does not make you a hopeless case. Actually, there is a thin line between the mental state of those who have found their bliss and those who have not. Externally, however, they are worlds apart because each group is judged by its creations. Those who have found their bliss are steadily realizing their goals. They are contributing to their world and are creating positive and beneficial results. Those who have not found this bliss, or True Purpose, are not experiencing the joy and fulfillment that comes with it.

Discovering your True Purpose and committing to it is both the beginning and the foundation of the mental state that will allow you to create the kind of life that you want. Look at it this way, your True Purpose is that broad spectrum on which all of your aspirations and potentialities lie. Your True Talent, which grows out of the True Purpose, is the tool to carry out your True Purpose, and your True Goal furthers, enhances and fulfills your True Purpose.

I believe that those people who go about life in an almost effortless manner and who continuously achieve great successes and accomplishments along the way are not charmed or lucky, but rather they have discovered and committed to their True Purpose. They have captured, embraced and have made use of their True Talent to accomplish their True Goal.

Determining True Purpose

Now let's focus on how you can determine your True Purpose. There are several approaches, but we will focus on only two of them: the Intuitive Process, which is a right brain function and includes non-dominant handwriting and drawing, and the Biographical Narrative which is a left brain function. Let us begin with the intuitive process.

Intuitive Process

This process involves various techniques for accessing your subconscious mind. Most of us have suppressed our knowledge of our True Purpose into the deep recesses of our subconscious mind. We have been told by society that individualism is rebellion and that we must conform to a particular norm. So we have laid layer upon layer of self-inhibiting rules and assumptions upon our True Purpose until we have lost conscious contact with it. But we know that it is there. That is why we experience the frustration of knowing we have a purpose, without being consciously aware of what that purpose is. So finding your True Purpose is really the process of bringing your subconscious mind into harmony with your conscious mind. Our awareness is the sum of our conscious and subconscious mind. There are many things that we are aware of, but not conscious of. For example, we are always aware of our breathing, heartbeat, pulse rate and the like, but we are not conscious of them until something calls them to our conscious attention. Until then, our awareness is subconscious.

The conscious mind is that part of your awareness that you are conscious of—your thoughts, feelings, ideas, etc. By contrast, you rarely know what is happening in your subconscious mind. But the thoughts, ideas, and feelings resident there—forgotten memories, repressed desires, unused information, suppressed knowledge—affect the way your mind works.

The Austrian physician Sigmund Freud was the first to recognize that there could be conflicts between conscious and subconscious thoughts, and he worked to bring the two into harmony through the use of various techniques. The technique most familiar to us is hypnosis, a temporary state of altered attention. You have perhaps heard stories of subjects who, under hypnosis, are able to recall things that happened early in childhood, experience changes in awareness, in creative imagination, in heart rate and in sensing cold and heat. That is simply the subconscious mind working. For centuries, hypnosis has been used to tap the subconscious mind, and its success is well documented.

Non-dominant Handwriting and Drawing

Other techniques that do some of the same things that hypnosis does—tap the subconscious—are writing and drawing with the non-dominant hand, which for 90 percent of the population is the left hand. To understand how this technique works, we should review the functions of the right brain.

The right brain is the intuitive hemisphere, often called the non-dominant part of our brain. The label of non-dominance is an archaic description given to the right brain when nearly all of research focused on the left brain, then called the logical brain. This focus resulted from our cultural bias toward logic, verbal and intellectual pursuits. The right brain with its mystic function was virtually ignored, but recent research involving right brain functions has clearly demonstrated the critical nature of right brain processing. The importance of right brain activity is so well documented now that the label of dominance vs. non-dominance is of no real value.

The right brain controls the left side of the body and the following functions.

1.   Imagery, visualization
2.   Holistic information processing, whereby it processes many types of information simultaneously
3.   Insight
4.   Spiritual experiences
5.   Artistic and creative abilities
6.   Entrance to subconscious mind

Studies have confirmed that when we write or draw with our non-dominant hand, we are accessing information by way of our right hemisphere, which is the pathway to our subconscious mind. Below the conscious level, we all know what our True Purpose is; we just need to peel back the layers of our conscious mind to recognize it. The non-dominant technique does that through both writing and drawing.

Biographical Narrative Technique

Another method of discovering your True Purpose is through the biographical narrative. This technique involves writing a brief narrative of the things that you want to accomplish. It is written as though it is dated sometime in the future when all of your goals have been achieved. From this narrative, you will be able to identify the major focus of your efforts and thereby identify your True Purpose.

As noted above, the biographical narrative is primarily a left brain approach. The left brain is your rational or logical brain and controls the right side of your body.

The left brain controls:
1. Verbal skills

2. Analytical and logical skills

3. Literal interpretation of words

4. Accessing and processing information sequentially

5. Processing number symbols and math functions

Because it is primarily a left brain approach, the biographical narrative is logical and analytical. It is based on the premise that high achievers are already pursuing their True Purpose, and that we can discover what that True Purpose is by analyzing both their accomplishments and focus in life.

Here's how this analysis works. Suppose the high achiever has a biographical entry in *Who's Who in the World* which describes his achievements, beliefs and attitudes. From this description, you could analyze what his True Purpose is in life.

Who's Who in the World

Aaron, Phillip. *Achievements*: Built a small commuter airline, Golden Pacific Airline, into a major international carrier. Wrote 45 bestsellers. Designed and manufactured an outstanding line of elegant, quality clothing for men. Created one of the world's best selling lines of perfume and cologne. Became a role model for young entrepreneurs. Gave generously to charities. Believed that success involved contributing to others. Inspired people to be the best they can be.

Two-Tier Approach

While both of these approaches—the non-dominant technique and the biographical narrative—are good and generally effective, each has its limitations. The approach presented here combines the best of both. It is a two-tier approach in which the exercises are done twice. The first time involves visualization and relaxation where you do these exercises in your imagination. The second time you will write and draw your answers.

The intent of this two-tier approach is to assist you in reaching deep inside yourself for your answers. By visualizing first, you are preparing your mind to yield information from a deeper level, ideally from your core. Both exercises should produce the same general pattern.

One word of caution before proceeding—you may want to do these exercises several times to achieve the best results. I can assure you that each time you do them, you will gain more clarity and insight.

Relaxation and Visualization Exercise

As noted above, this first exercise involves relaxation and visualization. You will need a tape recorder that you can use to record the exercise and play it back. First, read through the entire exercise; then record it. Next, find a place that is comfortable and where you can be alone, and play back the exercise. Let's get started.

Take a deep breath, holding it until the count of five, then open your mouth and let the air out.

Take another deep breath. Count 1 - 2 - 3 - 4 - 5 and let it go. Count 1 - 2 - 3 - 4 - 5 and take another deep breath. Count 1 - 2 - 3 - 4 - 5 and let it go.

Now as you continue to breathe deeply, imagine yourself lying on a beach on a quiet, sunny day. You are lying under a shade tree, and a warm breeze is flowing across your face and body. You hear the gentle lapping of the waves as the water comes up to the beach and, in the background, birds chirping overhead. These sounds all mix together into a relaxing, soothing and peaceful symphony.

Continue to breathe deeply. Count from 5 to 1 and on each descending count, go deeper and deeper.

> 5... going deeper
>
> 4... deeper
>
> 3... deeper
>
> 2... deeper yet
>
> 1... very deep

Now quiet your mind and your body and relax. Breathe deeply and relax.

As you go through these exercises, suspend all judgment and doubt. There are no impossibilities; there is nothing you cannot do if you truly want to do it.

Continue to breathe deeply and on each count from 5 to 1 go deeper and deeper. As you continue to breathe deeply, don't worry about trying to remember anything. Simply focus your mind on your breathing and your relaxation. Your subconscious mind will record, learn and properly use all the information you acquire here. As you count again from 5 to 1, feel yourself going deeper and deeper. 5 - 4 - 3 - 2 - 1 — breathing deeper.

Now imagine yourself lying there on the beach with a cool, gentle breeze flowing over your body, from your toes to your head. As it flows over your body, you continue to relax. First, this breeze blows over your right foot and then your left, and your feet relax. The breeze becomes warmer and gentler, soft and soothing. And now this warm, gentle, soft and soothing breeze moves from your right foot up over your right ankle, and up over your leg, over your knee, and all the way up over your thighs to your hip. As it moves up, the muscles in your right leg relax. Now this warm, gentle breeze moves down from your right hip over your thighs to your knees and down over your ankle to the tip of your toes, and your right leg becomes totally relaxed.

This breeze now moves over to your left leg. It is a warm, gentle, soft and soothing breeze that flows from your left ankle all the way to your thighs and up to your hip. Now both legs are totally relaxed.

This gentle breeze moves around the lower part of your body, up over your pelvis and around, and as it moves around, you relax more and more. The lower part of your body is now completely relaxed.

As you again count 5 to 1, you become more relaxed with each descending count. 5 going deeper; 4 - 3 going down; 2 very deep, and 1. Now this warm, gentle, soft and soothing breeze flows from your waist up the front of your body, going first over your stomach and relaxing it. It moves up over your chest, relaxing it. Then it moves all the way up to your shoulder and the base of your neck. You are totally relaxed now.

Now it moves from your right shoulder down your right arm to your elbow, down to your wrist and out to the tips of your fingers, relaxing your right arm. Then it moves from your left shoulder and down your left arm all the way to your elbow and then to your wrist and out to the tips of your fingers. You feel totally relaxed.

The breeze moves around to the back of your body and starting from your waist, it goes up your back. As it travels up your back all the way to your mid-back, the muscles relax and you go deeper and deeper. It moves up your back, over the mid-back, all the way to your shoulders, and you relax. This breeze goes all the way up over the top of your shoulders until it engulfs the base of your neck and you relax, going deeper and deeper. Now the upper part of your body is relaxed.

You relax even more with each descending count. 5 going deeper, 4 and deeper, 3 - 2 - and 1. Now this warm breeze circles your head and neck, and as it engulfs them with warm, soothing softness, you relax. Relax your face, focusing on your lips, your nose, your cheeks and your eyes. Then this breeze moves from your forehead and down the front of your face, past your eyes and nose, all the way down over your neck to its base and you relax. Then the breeze goes from the top of your head all the way down to the back of your head to where it connects to your neck, and you feel a wonderful release and relaxation as the tension flows out of your body.

Now this warm, gentle, soft and soothing breeze covers your entire body, moving from your head all the way down over your neck, your shoulders, both arms, your chest and back, your stomach and lower back. It moves all the way down your body over your thighs to your knees, and then over your lower legs to your ankles and both feet. Then it moves down the front of your body from your waist all the way down to your knees and your ankles and out the tips of your toes. Now you are totally relaxed. Stay with this peaceful feeling and experience the beauty of your relaxation.

As you relax, form a mental image of yourself lying out on the beach in a place that you like, under a shade tree, with the birds chirping and the sound of the waves in the background. As you lie there, you drift deeper into a wonderful, peaceful sleep. You feel secure and safe.

You begin to drift deeper into a dream that shows you your True Purpose in life. In your dream, you see yourself standing at the end of a white brick walkway. At the other end of the walkway is a large, beautiful golden mansion. You see yourself walking down the white brick walkway toward this beautiful golden mansion. With each step, you go down deeper and become more relaxed. 5 - 4 - 3 - 2 - 1.

As you approach the mansion, you see that it has a huge beautiful golden door. As you walk toward the door, you become more relaxed, more secure and safe with each step. When you reach it, the door gently swings open and you look inside. You see a long, beautifully lit hallway. On the right side of the hallway, there are three doors. You start walking down the hallway and approach the first door.

Above the first door is a sign which says, "True Purpose Writing Room, Non-dominant Hand." You open the door and feel yourself letting go because you feel safe and secure, and you sense no danger whatsoever. You relax totally. You enter the room, and on your right is a mahogany desk with a lighted lamp illuminating its surface. On the desk are a fountain pen and several sheets of paper. See yourself walk up behind the desk and pull back the soft leather chair and seat yourself. As you pull yourself up to the desk, you feel yourself going deeper and deeper and letting go more and more. You pick up the fountain pen and pull the paper towards you. Your name is written at the top of the paper, along with instructions which say, "Place the pen in your non-dominant hand and complete the statement below. The sentence reads, "My True Purpose in life is. . ."

With your non-dominant hand, you begin to write your True Purpose. As you write, you feel the answers coming from deep inside you, from your core. Your comfort, sense of certainty and your sense of destiny also grow. You complete this sentence, and you fold the paper and place it in your pocket. Then you get up and leave the room, feeling happy, relaxed, strong, confident and secure. At the door, you look back at the desk and chair, and you feel a sense of peace and accomplishment. You have definite knowledge of your destiny. You know your True Purpose. You know yourself.

You proceed down the hallway to the second door and there you find a sign above it that says, "True Purpose Drawing Room." You open the door and are greeted with a soft, gentle white light. It is the light of your creativity, and it is safe and comfortable. You feel very good. You feel very creative. You walk into the room. On your right, you see a drawing easel with a stool. Crayons, colored pencils and paints of every color are on the easel. There is a large sheet of art paper on the easel. At the top of the paper are your name and the following instructions, "Draw a picture of your True Purpose, using any of these tools that you wish."

You pick up a crayon, pencil, or brush—whichever you wish— and you start drawing a picture of your True Purpose. As you draw that picture, you feel yourself drawing with the core of your being, drawing with your True Purpose. With each stroke, your True Purpose becomes clearer and clearer. You continue drawing. You look at it and are pleased. Then you take your drawing, fold it, and leave the room.

You continue down the hallway until you reach the third door. There is a sign above it that says, "True Purpose Biographical Room." You enter the room and to your left you see another beautiful mahogany desk. A pen and several sheets of neatly stacked paper are on the desk. Both the desk and the chair are elevated, so you step up and sit at the desk. You pick up the pen and pull the paper to you. As you pull the paper towards you, you notice that your name is written at the top of the paper with the following instructions: "Assume it is 20 years from today and you are writing a brief description of yourself and your accomplishments." You begin to write and you feel yourself connecting with your core.

Now to do this, think about a time in the future, say the year 2020. Think about the things you would look for and the things you would look at to determine what your life purpose has been. Write all the things you have done that illustrate your life purpose. Relax and go deeper and deeper. Now, go back to the paper and start to write as though it were the year 2020 and you are writing out the things that show your True Purpose in life. As you write, you feel yourself connecting with your core and your true self. You are not writing with your hand, nor with your conscious mind, but you are writing with the essence of your true self. At the bottom of the page, you conclude by writing, "Therefore my True Purpose is. . ." and complete the sentence. You take the paper, fold it and put it in your pocket, and you leave the room.

Walk out of the mansion and back to the beach where you lie down under the shade tree. Then you feel that warm, gentle breeze again and you find yourself totally relaxed. Now you know that it is time to end this exercise so you feel energy coming back into your body. Then when you count from 1 to 5, you will awake feeling totally energized, happy, relaxed and secure. 1 - coming up, 2 - feeling the energy coming into your body, 3 - more energy, 4 - feeling alert and energized, and 5 - fully awake.

Take a few minutes to reflect on your experience. Remember you will experience more clarity and insight the more you do this exercise.

It is a good idea to do this exercise at least three times during a 30-day self-discovery program. I should hasten to add, however, that the frequency with which you do the exercise should depend on how you feel about the validity of the information you obtain.

True Purpose Exercises

The second tier of these exercises involves writing and drawing. Worksheets have been provided for you on pages 157-160. I have also provided two sets of completed worksheets as a guide for you. See pages 149-156.

First, with your non-dominant hand, write the completion of the statement, "My True Purpose is..." After you have finished your statement, draw a picture of your True Purpose with your non-dominant hand. Finally, write your biographical narrative as you wish it to be in the year 2020 or so.

Then ask yourself the following questions.

1.   When you wrote out "My True Purpose is..." with your non-dominant hand, did you feel like you had done it before?

2.   When you drew the picture, did you feel that you were drawing a picture you had seen before?

3.   When you wrote out your biographical narrative did you feel like you were writing things you had seen, heard or thought about before?

4.   When you concluded writing your life purpose with your non-dominant hand, how did you feel? Did you feel a sense of:
     • Direction
     • Confidence
     • Higher self-esteem
     • Determination

5.   When you drew the picture, did you feel a sense of direction? Did you also feel a sense of:
     • Determination
     • Confidence
     • Higher self-esteem

6.   When you wrote the biographical narrative, did you feel a sense of direction? Did you also feel a sense of:
    • Confidence
    • Determination
    • Higher self-esteem

Sample
NON-DOMINANT HANDWRITING
True Purpose

Name *Phillip Richard Aaron*

Place your pen in your left hand (right hand if you are left-handed), and complete the following sentence.

My True Purpose in life is.... *To apply music in a way to change People's lives and to improve relations in an indifferent world.*

Sample
NON-DOMINANT DRAWING
True Purpose

Name *Phillip Richard Aaron*

Using your non-dominant hand, draw a picture of your True Purpose.

Sample
BIOGRAPHICAL NARRATIVE
True Purpose

Name *Phillip Richard Aaron*

TAKING the world by storm a little over 4 years ago, Phillip Richard Aaron has been deemed the "world's brightest hope" for a peaceful future. In 1993, he released his first album and since then has been spellbinding people with his lyrical messages.

The recipient of many awards from various national leaders, he has helped ease the tension of many hostile countries. He has become a very prominent businessman since retiring from the stresses of a performer in late 1996. From his international chain of record stores to his restaurant franchise on the west coast, he is listed in Forbes Magazine as one of the top 15 millionares in the U.S.

Based on his accomplishments and presentations in life, *Phillip Richard Aaron*'s True Purpose or mission in life is:

to be a successful musician who changes the world with powerful musical statements and sounds.

Sample
TRUE PURPOSE
STATEMENT SUMMARY

Name _Phillip Richard Aaron_

1. **Non-dominant Writing** *My purpose in life is to apply music in a way to change people's lives and to improve relations in an indifferent world.*
2. **Non-dominant Drawing** *My purpose in life is to use music as an opening to people's hearts and bring about a change in the world's methods by bringing peace and harmony openly.*
3. **Biographical Narrative**

    My purpose in life is to be a successful musician who changes the world through powerful musical statements and sounds.

Using all three of the above statements, write your True Purpose in life statement.

My True Purpose in life is... *to be the best musician and help the world & its people by bringing about a positive change through music.*

Sample
NON-DOMINANT HANDWRITING
True Purpose

Name _BE+A HANFORD_

Place your pen in your left hand (right hand if you are left-handed), and complete the following sentence.

My True Purpose in life is...

to HELP PEOPLE GET THE
BEST OUT OF LIFE

Sample
NON-DOMINANT DRAWING
True Purpose

Name _BETH HANFORD_

Using your non-dominant hand, draw a picture of your True Purpose.

Sample
BIOGRAPHICAL NARRATIVE
True Purpose

Name **BETH HANFORD**

BETH HAS ASSISTED IN WORKSHOPS AND SEMINARS THROUGHOUT HER LIFE MAKING HER LIFE AND THOUSANDS OF OTHERS PEOPLE'S LIVES THE BEST THEY CAN BE. SHE HAS TRAVELED to MANY PLACES DOING THIS. HELPING MANY PEOPLE ACHIEVE THEIR BEST AND HAS SATISFIED HER DESIRE FOR KNOWLEDGE OF DIFFERENT CULTURES IN DOING SO. SHE HAS OPENED HOMES FOR CATS AND HAS ASSISTED IN HELPING OTHERS DO THE SAME AND THEREFORE HAS CONTINUED HER LOVE OF ANIMALS. SHE HAS SURROUNDED HERSELF IN HER LIFE by PEOPLE WHO ARE DESIRING THE BEST OUT OF LIFE.

Based on her accomplishments and presentations in life, **BETH**'s True Purpose or mission in life is:

TO HELP PEOPLE GET THE BEST OUT OF LIFE

Sample
TRUE PURPOSE
STATEMENT SUMMARY

Name _BethHanford_

1. **Non-dominant Writing** *MY PURPOSE IN LIFE IS TO HELP PEOPLE GET THE BEST OUT OF LIFE*

2. **Non-dominant Drawing** *MY PURPOSE IN LIFE IS TO ASSIST PEOPLE THROUGH SEMINARS AND GENUINE CARING OF ALL PEOPLE, TO ACHIEVE THEIR BEST IN LIFE.*

3. **Biographical Narrative**
MY PURPOSE IN LIFE IS TO ASSIST PEOPLE THROUGHOUT THE WORLD TO GET THE BEST OUT OF LIFE AND TO HELP ALL ANIMALS IN THE WORLD HAVE THE BEST LIVES POSSIBLE

Using all three of the above statements, write your True Purpose in life statement.

My True Purpose in life is... *to HELP PEOPLE ACHIEVE THE BEST OUT OF LIFE*

NON-DOMINANT HANDWRITING
True Purpose

Name _____

Place your pen in your left hand (right hand if you are left-handed), and complete the following sentence.

My True Purpose in life is. . . .

NON-DOMINANT DRAWING
True Purpose

Using your non-dominant hand, draw a picture of your True Purpose.

BIOGRAPHICAL NARRATIVE
True Purpose

Based on his accomplishments and presentations in life, _____'s True Purpose or mission in life is:

TRUE PURPOSE STATEMENT SUMMARY

1. **Non-dominant Writing**
   My purpose in life is. . .

2. **Non-dominant Drawing**
   My purpose in life is. . .

3. **Biographical Narrative**
   My purpose in life is. . .

Using all three of the above statements, write your True Purpose in life statement.

My True Purpose in life is. . .

Having taken you through the exercises for determining your True Purpose, I want to review some of the information that I have given you by summarizing it into three questions.

1. How will you know when you have discovered your True Purpose?

- All three processes—writing and drawing your True Purpose and writing your biographical narrative—will yield the same result or at least a pattern will emerge.

- You will feel a sense of focus, centeredness, destiny, enthusiasm, clarity and determination.

- You will have self-confidence and courage.

- You will clarify your decision-making process, making all decisions on the basis of whether they further your True Purpose.

- You will have a strong sense of focus and commitment that adds up to magnetic personality.

2. How will others know that you have discovered your True Purpose?

- They will be drawn to you.

- They will recognize your commitment and focus.

- They will respect your commitment.

- By knowing where you stand, they will feel a sense of security in dealing with you.

3. What will be the internal benefit to you of knowing and committing to your True Purpose?

- Knowing and committing to your True Purpose creates an internal state that allows you to create exactly what you want externally. That is, you will have created a foundation for reaching your True Goal and using your True Talent.

- You will feel guided by your True Purpose

- You will have an internal strength and peace.

- You will experience joy and fulfillment.

Conclusion of True Purpose

Having completed the exercises for determining your True Purpose, it is now time to analyze your findings. As you review the True Purpose exercises, you should look for areas of commonality. The relaxation and visualization exercises are designed to facilitate the flow of information from your subconscious mind. In reflecting on these exercises, recall whether your responses lead toward the same general conclusions. This is not to suggest, however, that each of the exercises will lead to the same conclusion. You may have visualized a different purpose in one of the exercises. Don't be discouraged if you did because that simply means that you either have more than one strong inclination—in which case you must decide which one is paramount—or that you need to look more carefully for a pattern. In either case, reviewing the balance of the exercises will lead to greater clarity.

Next, review the actual exercises. Determine whether they are consistent with each other and whether they are consistent with the relaxation and visualization exercises. If they are, then you have identified your True Purpose. The important thing here is to identify a general pattern. If one has not emerged, or if you feel uncomfortable with the one that has emerged, then repeat the exercise until you are satisfied as to the validity of the results. When you feel confident that you have identified your True Purpose, move on to identify your True Talent.

IDENTIFYING YOUR TRUE TALENT

Definition of True Talent

You have a skill at which you are exceptionally good. Perhaps you have been fortunate enough to identify this skill, or you may be still searching for it. Whatever the case, it is quite possible that, like most of us, you are not in a job or career that allows you to use this skill. And, again, like most of us, you may have let jobs, positions and others dictate which skill you develop or focus on. This is, in fact, the opposite of what you should do.

To be the best that you can be, you should first discover your True Talent, and then allow it to guide you to your True Goal. Bear in mind that by True Talent, I am talking about that one single skill that surpasses all other talents that you have.

You may have several other talents that support your True Goal, but you have one True Talent. It is a skill that is second nature to you. It flows effortlessly from you and is the one that you enjoy doing and using the most.

Your True Talent enables you to be the best that you can be. It is that ability which, when used, gives you fulfillment. It is, in short, what you do best. It may be the ability to organize, to motivate, to build, to write, to draw, to speak. Whatever it is, it is a specific, clearly definable and recognizable skill, and it is an outgrowth of your True Purpose.

Discovering Your True Talent

Your True Purpose forms the foundation of all you can be. From it, emerge your True Talent and then your True Goal. At first glance, this sequence appears illogical, and you may wonder why True Talent should precede True Goal. Your analysis may go something like this: "It seems reasonable to find out what you really want to do in life (True Goal) and then to apply whatever talents you have to achieving it. Therefore, starting with True Goal would be more reasonable and more analytically correct."

Although that is certainly a reasonable approach, it is not the most effective one. Look at it this way, once you have identified your True Purpose, a whole range of possibilities emerges, revealing a number of appropriate vehicles that you can use to satisfy your True Purpose. The issue then becomes which of these possibilities, or range of appropriate vehicles, represents your True Goal? If your True Purpose is to eliminate hunger in the world, then the range of possibilities is broad. You could, for example, choose to pursue your purpose by becoming a farmer and add to the world's food supply. Or you could become a politician and use your political influence and power to change the policies affecting hunger. Or you could become a scientist and use your research abilities to develop sturdier food crops.

Let's assume that your True Talent is in dealing with and influencing people and policies. In that case and in the range of possibilities in our example, your True Goal would be to become a politician, not a farmer. So not only should True Talent precede the determination of True Goal, but an efficient and effective analysis demands that it precede. When you identify and start with your True Talent, your True Goal will naturally follow.

So while it may appear on the surface that you are giving little or no concern to selecting a goal you would like to pursue, the contrary is true. By identifying your True Talent, you will be moving toward your True Goal, which is the specific thing you ought to be doing, because it is the thing you are best equipped to do. True Talent leads you to that goal, the achievement of which brings you joy and fulfillment. So this approach does not ignore your desires and wants, it simply takes them into account as internal components of our analysis.

True Talent Questions

You may recall that in the discussion of True Purpose, three questions helped you understand the nature, affect and power of True Purpose. Now I am going to make minor adjustments to those questions and ask them again.

1. Under True Purpose, we asked whether you felt you are on this planet for a reason. Most people do believe this. As a follow-up to that question in regard to True Talent, allow me to ask:

   Since you are on this planet for a reason, do you believe that you have been given the talent to realize that reason?

2. Also under True Purpose, we asked whether you felt that you have a purpose in life. Most people believe their lives have purpose.

   Since you feel that you have a purpose in life, do you feel that you have been given the talent to accomplish that purpose?

Doesn't it make sense if you have a True Purpose in life, that the Source of the purpose would also provide you the talent to realize it? Having a True Purpose would not make sense otherwise; it would be like commanding a bird to fly and then clipping its wings. That would be a cruel hoax to play on humanity and nature simply does not work that way.

3. Finally, I asked if you knew what your purpose in life is. Most people indicate that they do not know. As a follow-up, consider this question:

   Do you know what your True Talent is?

In life, you are surrounded by one unavoidable law—the law of things moving from a beginning to an end. Everything around you has some purpose and function that is woven into the overall purpose and function of nature. You know that you, too, have a purpose, and you know that you have the talent for achieving this purpose. But, perhaps, you are frustrated because you have not yet discovered what that talent is.

The exercises in this book are designed to help you rid yourself of this frustration by showing you how to find the life you ought to be living.

The Hallmark of Great Accomplishments

True Talent is the hallmark of all great accomplishments. When President Kennedy set a goal of putting a man on the moon, the National Aeronautics and Space Administration (NASA) went about its goal of finding the best, most talented people to serve in the astronaut program. They matched each one of those persons with others whose talents they complemented.

Thomas Edison's True Talent was that of creative genius. One of the greatest inventors in history, he used his genius to create and patent more than 1,100 inventions in 60 years. Many of these inventions revolutionized the quality of our lives.

Another man revolutionized modern life when he chose between what looked like two True Talents. A gifted painter, George Washington Carver chose instead to follow his natural curiosity about plant life. He made more than 300 products from the peanut, including printer's ink, face powder, soap, milk substitute. His True Talent was such genius that he won international fame for his agricultural research.

Leonardo Da Vinci was one of the most versatile geniuses in history, and one of the greatest painters of the Italian Renaissance, giving us the famous *Mona Lisa* and *The Last Supper*. An excellent observer, he concentrated on what the eye could see, rather than on abstract thoughts. And his powers of observation led him to study anatomy, astronomy, botany, and geology. As an outgrowth of these studies, he designed machines and drew plans for hundreds of inventions, some of which were centuries before their time. For example, he designed an airplane and a parachute.

Albert Einstein's True Talent was that of scientific genius. When he was 26 years old, he presented three papers which changed the study of physics: 1) On *quanta*, which said that light was a stream of tiny particles. This paper became the basis of the "electric eye" and made possible sound motion pictures and television; 2) On *Relativity* which showed the equivalence of mass and energy; 3) On *Brownian motion* which confirmed the atomic theory of matter.

Duke Ellington discovered his True Talent in music. He ranks as one of the greatest jazz musicians in history, giving us such songs as

"Mood Indigo," "Solitude," and "In a Sentimental Mood." Together with the Ellington Band, which he directed, he regularly gave jazz concerts. He introduced a major new composition at Carnegie Hall each year between 1943 and 1950; the most famous of these compositions was "Black, Brown and Beige."

Using his True Talent of teaching and influencing others, Booker T. Washington founded, in 1881, what is now Tuskegee University. Under his leadership, the school became a model of industrial education. He became a shrewd political leader and advised presidents, members of congress, and governors, becoming the most influential black leader of his time.

Each of these men was a giant in his field of talent, but there are other giants who have followed their True Talent—some achieving fame and others not. Throughout the world, talented men and women pursue their True Purpose, using their True Talents: talented mechanics make engines hum smoothly; talented teachers challenge students to reach higher; talented draftsmen draw plans for buildings, bridges, machines; talented social workers put lives back together; talented singers fill choirs or make recordings that inspire; talented parents instill solid values in their children. The world is filled with talented people who fulfill their True Purpose in all sorts of jobs—the secret is finding your True Talent.

There is no doubt in my mind that True Talent is, indeed, the hallmark of all great accomplishments. You have heard stories of people who pursued one talent and who, in the process, discovered another talent which was for more important than the one they pursued. You may think that such a discovery was the result of an accident. I disagree, because the result of a person's living his True Purpose is that it will lead him to things he ought to be doing. The things he does are never a result of an accident.

You, too, may be looking for one thing, but if you continue to follow your interests, you will eventually discover what your natural gifts and talents are. Ask yourself these questions. What do I do well? What interests me? What gives me the most joy? What energizes me? Discovering your True Talent is an indispensable part of optimum living—that is, living the life you ought to be living.

Connecting True Talent to True Purpose

Your True Talent flows naturally from your True Purpose. Earlier,

I told you that True Purpose is a broad continuum that includes a range of possibilities, on which is your True Talent. You cannot commit to and discover your True Purpose without placing yourself on that continuum and, thereby, gaining access to your True Talent. But you do not get an automatic revelation of your True Talent when you commit to your True Purpose. It requires further analysis and testing. The following questions are part of that discovery process.

What does it mean to follow your True Talent?

You will know that you are following your True Talent when whatever you do is done exceedingly well, when it gives you fulfillment, and when you joyfully create things that are consistent with your True Purpose in life.

How do you know when you have discovered your True Talent?

The answer to this question really has two components. The first deals with the *technique* used to determine your True Talent, and the second deals with your *emotional state* after you have discovered your True Talent.

Let's look first at the technique component.

Technique Component

The three techniques for discovering your True Talent are similar to the ones under True Purpose. As you recall, you used: non-dominant handwriting, non-dominant drawing, and the biographical narrative. When your responses to these three techniques lined up and generally pointed in the same direction, you had confirmation of your True Purpose. You will use the same approach to discover your True Talent.

Emotional State Component

The emotional state component checks whether your feelings about the discovery of your True Talent line up with the results of these three techniques.

Here are some feelings or emotional reactions you should have when you discover your Talent.

1. Your self-esteem will rise.
2. You will feel enthusiastic about using your True Talent.

3. You will feel confident of your ability to exercise, and/or learn to exercise, your True Talent.
4. You will feel a sense of clarity and certainty about your talent.
5. You will experience the same joy and satisfaction when you use your True Talent for work or play.

You may not experience these feelings simultaneously, or even immediately upon discovering your True Talent. But you will experience them. And when you do, you can rest assured that you have discovered and committed to your True Talent.

How will others know when you have discovered and committed to your True Talent?

The answer to this question also has two components. The first deals with the receptivity of others to your emotional reaction, and the second with others' observation of your external manifestation of your True Talent.

Receptivity of Others

As you follow your True Talent, others will observe the following:

1. Your enthusiasm, and they will describe you as being enthusiastic.
2. Your confidence, your clarity, your certainty and your heightened self-esteem, and they will describe you that way.
3. Your enjoyment of exercising your True Talent, and they will describe you as one who loves what he is doing.

External Manifestation

Others will observe that as you exercise your True Talent you are:

1. More productive
2. Effortlessly accomplishing goals
3. More motivated
4. Less procrastinating
5. More efficient in your actions
6. More effective
7. Experiencing genuine joy

Finally, they will see and recognize your True Talent.

How does exercising your True Talent lead to success?

There is an essential linkage between True Purpose, True Talent and True Goal. If you have discovered both your True Purpose and your True Talent, the next step is to manifest them externally. You do this through creating exactly what you want; in other words, through creating success. The exercise of your True Talent is doing the thing you do best, and that leads to success. When you are living the life you ought to be living, pursuing the goal you ought to be pursuing, and exercising your True Talent, you automatically draw people and resources to yourself so that you can continue to do the things that you ought to be doing. The result is pure success.

True Talent Exercises

The following exercises will help you identify your True Talent. You will recognize them as the same exercises that you did under True Purpose: non-dominant writing, non-dominant drawing, and a biographical narrative. The focus of the exercises has narrowed considerable here, however. As you explore your True Talent, your aim is to be more specific than you were on your True Purpose exercises. Please do the exercises now.

NON-DOMINANT HANDWRITING
True Talent

Place your pen in your left hand (right hand if you are left-handed), and complete the following sentence.

My True Talent in life is. . .

NON-DOMINANT DRAWING
True Talent

Using your non-dominant hand, draw a picture of your True Talent.

BIOGRAPHICAL NARRATIVE
True Talent

Based on his/her accomplishments and presentations in life, _____'s True Talent in life is:

TRUE TALENT STATEMENT SUMMARY

1. Non-dominant Writing
My True Talent in life is...

2. Non-dominant Drawing
My True Talent in life is...

3. Biographical Narrative
My True Talent in life is...

Using all three of the above statements, write your True Talent in life statement.

My True Talent in life is...

Summary of True Talent

By now you should have identified both your True Purpose and your True Talent, and you should be experiencing a sense of confidence, direction, focus and a heightened self-esteem because of your commitment to them. You have now begun to create the internal state necessary to create exactly what you want externally. The final step in this process is to identify and commit to your True Goal.

IDENTIFYING YOUR TRUE GOAL

Introduction

This book is about power! That inner power that creates the kind of future you want and deserve. This inner power comes from and has its seed in your True Purpose. Look at True Purpose as the ground in which your True Talent is rooted, and your True Goal as the tree that grows from the roots out of that ground. There can be no roots without the ground, and certainly no tree without the roots. Having laid the ground and planted the roots, you are now at the point of growing your tree. It is time to discover your True Goal.

Definition of True Goal

True Goal is that specific objective that satisfies your True Purpose and maximizes the effectiveness and efficiency of your True Talent. While both True Purpose and True Talent are tied to your True Goal, True Talent has the most direct impact on the narrowing and focusing process that leads to your True Goal.

Remember that True Purpose is a continuum along which there are many talents that may be used to satisfy your True Purpose. The same could be said of your True Goal. Along the continuum of True Purpose are many goals, but not all of them are best suited for you. The yardstick for measuring which is best suited for you is simply whether a goal allows you to be the best that you can be. Your True Talent helps you narrow this choice and, therefore, has a direct and immediate effect on your discovering your True Goal.

Using the example that we used earlier, suppose your True Purpose is to eradicate hunger. The goals along this continuum may include:

1. To be a politician and use your power to eradicate hunger.
2. To be a philanthropist and donate large sums to organizations that feed the poor.
3. To be a farmer and grow crops that you give to the needy.

Now let's assume that your True Talent is the ability to influence people and to speak before groups in ways that motivate them to take action. Obviously, you could use this talent to meet a number of different goals. Your True Goal will be the area that allows you to use your True Talent to be the best that you can be. If your True Purpose is to eradicate hunger and your True Talent is to influence and motivate people, then it follows that the most effective and efficient use of your True Talent, among the choices that we have given, would be to become a politician. You can see from this example that your True Goal is that option that allows the most efficient, effective and productive use of your True Talent.

True Goal Questions

The questions raised by this part of our discussion are like those raised earlier for True Purpose and True Talent. And like the earlier ones, their answers lead to a better understanding of the topic at hand— True Goal.

How do you discover your True Goal?

The techniques used here are generally like those used before. First, do the non-dominant handwriting, the non-dominant drawing, and the biographical narrative. Then match up each of these to determine whether they are in harmony.

An additional step in this analysis is to determine whether your True Goal is in harmony with your True Purpose, and whether it flows naturally and logically from your True Purpose and your True Talent.

How do you know when you have discovered your True Goal?

As I have indicated above, the results of all your exercises should line up. For example, look at the emotional component. When you have discovered your True Goal, you will feel a sense of destiny. You will not only know what you ought to be doing, but you will know you have the talent to accomplish it. This knowledge will give you more self-confidence and self-esteem. The fact that you know what you ought to be doing and that you know you have the talent to do it also gives you a tremendous sense of power.

Motivation in its purest form follows; you will do things that lead you to your True Goal effortlessly and in a manner that is second nature. Your motivation and action merge. You have a confidence that does not require boasting; it will speak for itself.

How will others know that you have discovered your True Goal?

The answers here are basically the same as those under True Talent and True Purpose. Others will:

- Be drawn to you
- Recognize your commitment and focus
- Respect your commitment
- Feel a sense of security in dealing with you because they know where you stand

True Goal Exercises

This is one of the most exciting parts of this entire book because here is where you discover your True Goal. Do the writing, the drawing and the biographical narrative exercises. They will lead you to and help you discover your True Goal.

After doing the exercises, you will find that your resolve to pursue your True Goal is stronger than ever before. The security of knowing that you can be the best you can be by committing to and following your True Goal will motivate you to live the life you ought to be living. The result is power—the power to create.

NON-DOMINANT HANDWRITING
True Goal

Place your pen in your left hand (right hand if you are left-handed), and complete the following sentence.

My True Goal in life is...

NON-DOMINANT DRAWING
True Goal

Using your non-dominant hand, draw a picture of your True Goal.

BIOGRAPHICAL NARRATIVE
True Goal

Based on his/her accomplishments and presentations in life, _____'s True Goal in life is:

TRUE GOAL STATEMENT SUMMARY

1. Non-dominant Writing
My True Goal in life is...

2. Non-dominant Drawing
My True Goal in life is...

3 Biographical Narrative
My True Goal in life is...

Using all three of the above statements, write your True Goal in life statement.

My True Goal in life is...

Summary of True Goal

By now you have discovered your True Goal. Perhaps this is the first time you have given this amount of thought to determining your True Goal. There is no doubt that you are goal-oriented or you would not be reading this book. I would venture to say, however, that in the past, you have not attempted to line up your True Talent with your True Goal in the way you have just done. No doubt your exploration of your True Purpose has been even rarer. In the last few hours, you have done something that most people go through life without ever doing. That fact alone will put you significantly ahead of most of the population.

Discovering your True Purpose, your True Talent and your True Goal gives you the inner power to create exactly what you want. Remember, what you *want* to create is what you *ought* to create, and what you ought to create maximizes your True Talent and leads to the achievement of your True Goal—to the life you ought to be living, and the activity you ought to be doing.

You have created the inner power. Now let's apply what you have learned.

TWO
LEARNING TO EMPOWER
YOUR GOAL

UNDERSTANDING HOW TO EMPOWER GOALS

Empowering Your Goals

Y ou have set the stage and put everything in place. You have identified and committed to your True Purpose, your True Talent and your True Goal. You have completed the first step in developing the internal state that allows you to create what you want. Now you are ready to move to the second step in this creation process, the empowering of your goal.

Getting from here to the actual realization of your goal requires more than just having the enabling state. It requires action. As Bishop A.L. Hardy says, "Knowing how to get to Tacoma doesn't get you there. You have to go."

People who accomplish great things seem to have several things in common. The most revealing thing that emerges from this commonality is how they deal with their goals. The often quoted Harvard Study reveals that those graduates that had written financial goals had met or exceeded them in five years. The study also showed that those with written goals made more money than those without written goals.

Corporations now make it a standard practice to set written goals to aim at and to measure their progress. Study after study has shown that goal setting is crucial to success in any field. The following section deals with goal setting and the empowering of your goals through the process of vibrant and dynamic experiencing called sensory-rich visualization.

DEVELOPING SKILLS FOR EMPOWERING

Goal Setting

The goal is the target of all effectively directed action, and goal setting is your map to success. Without goals, every direction seems right, or perhaps wrong. Without goals, you do not know where you are going, and you certainly can't tell when you get there. Without goal setting, all of our discoveries, accomplishments and conquests would be accidental occurrences left to the probability of chance. Without goals, the world would be a much different place, and man certainly would not have a basis for claiming to be the highest species.

Imagine, if you will, a world left to chance. Chaos would be its ruler. Patterns, standards and guidelines would be non-existent, and life would be virtually hell on earth.

Goal setting brings order into your life. It allows you to build on both past successes and failures. It sets time-lines, targets and measurements. It gives you confidence, because well-defined goals properly planned and executed lead to their accomplishment. Success is, indeed, a product of goal setting.

Every plan must have an objective, and this applies to every facet of your life. Goal setting is an indispensable part part of a life that follows your True Purpose, that makes use of your True Talent and that accomplishes your True Goal. It is inherent in the creation process.

Principles of Goal Setting

The rules for goal setting have been run up the flag pole so many times that they have become suspect. Many people doubt their validity because it appears that the application of the rules has not worked for many of us. However, it is not the failure of the rules, but the improper application of and the failure to follow them that cause the concern.

The rules of goal setting work and have been validated in several studies. Often graduates of some courses that teach these rules judge them harshly because, over the long term, they have not actually accomplished their goals. This judgment comes because their expectations differed from the objective of the course. Most of us attended goal setting seminars expecting to learn how to accomplish goals. The seminar's objective was to teach us how to set the goals, not how to accomplish them. You and I determine whether the goal setting rules work by whether we accomplish our goals.

Goal setting is just one step toward achievement. From there, you must empower your goals and implement your plans. So when you look at goal setting as a measure of the effectiveness of goal accomplishment, you start the analysis before the process is completed.

Much more than goal setting is required to succeed. Once goals are set, something must take them from your mind to reality. Empowering your goals is the mechanism that begins the creative process, and the well-planned execution of your success strategy is the culmination of the process.

This entire section deals with empowering your goals. Here you will learn not only proper goal setting, but also how to visualize and affirm those goals in a congruent and harmonious manner. The rules for goal setting are simple and have been validated time and time again. They are:

1. Goals should be in writing. The Harvard Study showed that those who write their goals are more likely to accomplish them than those who do not write them. Written goals have a powerful inherent effect upon us. Part of this power stems from the fact that the act of writing the goal is, in and of itself, part of the creation process.

Think of it this way, the great cathedrals and the classical masterpieces all began as a concept in their creators' minds. The act of taking that concept and placing it on paper is one step along the creation process, and it eventually results in the actual construction of the building or the performance of the composition.

The fact that the concept has moved from the mind to written form means that it has left the invisible mental world and entered the visible physical world. Because you merely placed the concept on paper, the creative process is further along the way.

2. Goals should be result-oriented. Your goal should state in positive and concrete terms the result you want to create. The primary focus of the statement should be the desired outcome. For example, if you desire to have a net worth of $1 million, your goal statement should read: *My goal is to have a net worth of $1 million.* Note that this is different from an affirmation statement which is written as though it had already been achieved.

Goal statements written as complex or compound sentences are probably not very effective, and they certainly are not as effective as the simple direct statement just given.

3. Use only positive words in describing your goal. Goal setting is aimed at getting a specific result. A negative statement does not target a specific result; it targets a condition or situation that you seek to avoid. The negatively stated goal is confusing to the subconscious mind. For example, a goal "not to fail" has no specific target. Laughingly, you may say that is often your goal. But any effort not to fail is really an effort to succeed at something. If you state your goal positively, your subconscious mind can efficiently concentrate on helping you achieve the goal. A negatively stated goal does not always contain obvious red flags. Some come disguised as positive goals. The following example illustrates this.

> **Positive:** My goal is to have a net worth of $1 million by January 1995.

> **Negative:** My goal is to be worth not less than $1 million by January 1995.

Specificity—measurable and time specific— will guard against negative goals.

4. Goals should be time specific. Your goals must have a realistic time target. The time target not only provides a tool by which you can judge how well you are moving toward your goal and tells you when you accomplish it, but it also helps you to plan and to execute your goal-oriented plans.

We could time target the goal statement in our previous example by adding a specific date: My goal is to have a net worth of $1 million *on January 30, 1995.*

5. Your goal must be measurable. This element of your goal statement is a natural outcome of the other principles we have discussed. You must have a means of measuring your goal so that you will know not only when you reach it, but also how well you are doing along the way. The measurable part of the goal statement we have been working with is the $1 million and January 30, 1995. You can measure your progress; you can know when you are a quarter of the way to the goal, or halfway, or three-quarters of the way. When you include a measurable, or countable, element to the goal, you have a measuring tool to guide your progress.

Summary

To summarize, your goals should be:

1. Written

2. Result-oriented

3. Positive

4. Time specific

5. Measurable

CREATING THE INTERNAL STATE
THAT EMPOWERS

Visualization

E arlier, I briefly mentioned the need to bring the conscious and subconscious mind into harmony with each other. This agreement is absolutely essential in order for you to consistently create what you want. Visualization, the component of the empowering process that you are about to learn, is the most effective and powerful way of creating this agreement that I have come across.

But to understand how and why visualization works, you need to look at the issue of reality and the subconscious mind. If information is presented in a believable format, the subconscious processes it as though it were true. This has long been demonstrated by hypnosis. Subjects under hypnosis have reacted physically to conditions described to them, even though the conditions did not exist. In some experiments, the subject's skin blistered after suggestions of heat, and the subject visibly trembled from chill after suggestions of cold.

The examples go on and on until there is no room for reasonably questioning the power of the subconscious mind to produce responses based upon unreal, yet dynamically perceived conditions. In short, the subconscious mind will accept fiction as fact. The only limitation appears to be how the material is presented.

Its inability to distinguish between fact and fiction makes the subconscious both a positive and negative agent. The negative is that your personality may be damaged by events, conditions and experiences that exist only within the walls of your subconscious mind.

The positive is that you can present conditions to the subconscious mind the way you would like for them to be, and your subconscious will react as though those things were true. An obvious question arises when we describe the reaction of the subconscious mind in this way: If the subconscious believes everything, why doesn't it believe me when I tell it that I am happy, successful and prosperous?

The subconscious mind doesn't believe everything presented to it; it simply has the capability of doing so under certain conditions. Whatever is presented to it must be packaged in a way that is acceptable to the subconscious mind's belief system. In other words, whatever is presented must be believable.

To be believable to the subconscious mind, an idea must have sensory characteristics as though it were true. It must have the quality of sensory richness. Sight, sound, touch, taste, smell and emotions must be included in its presentation.

Through sensory-rich visualization, you develop a life-like quality for your goals and create a sense of realism which your subconscious mind accepts as true. Once that happens, and assuming that you are consciously committed to your goal, your subconscious and conscious minds come into harmony, and the result is pure creative power.

Sensory-Rich Description

To give your goal the dynamic, vibrant and powerful quality of sensory richness, describe it in a way that allows the subconscious mind to experience it as though it were being perceived through the senses—visualized.

Some people believe they cannot visualize because they have trouble developing the sought-after image. So they settle for "a strong impression" in lieu of a sensory-rich image. The strong impression, however, cannot create the desired results because it lacks the required sensory richness needed to be accepted by the subconscious mind.

Sensory-rich visualization, not a strong impression, is absolutely critical to the process of empowering your goals. A review of the purpose of visualization makes this abundantly clear.

1. It creates a sensory-rich visual target and enables you to see it clearly enough to know whether you have hit it.

2. The sensory-rich image contantly reminds you that you can accomplish your goal and motivates you to do so.

Everyone can and does visualize. Sometimes, and with some things, we do it better than at other times with other things. Fortunately, all of us can learn to visualize in a stronger, clearer image. All we need do is describe the thing we want to visualize in a sensory-rich form as though it has occurred. Let's look at the elements of a sensory-rich description of your goal.

The first element of your sensory-rich image is SIGHT. Describe how your accomplished goal will look.

1. Describe its size
2. Describe its color
3. Describe its shape
4. Describe its location
5. Describe its surroundings.
6. Describe its motion
7. Place yourself in the description.

By making your goal life size and giving it color and motion, and by placing yourself in the picture, you create a stronger, more pleasant visual image.

Now let's assume that your goal is to purchase and fully pay for a beautiful mansion. Let's have some fun and describe it, using the approach we just outlined.

1. How is it shaped?
2. How many bedrooms do you want in the house?
3. How many floors?
4. Describe the doors, the windows and the like.
5. What color is it?
6. What colors are the curtains, the carpets?
7. Where are you in the picture?
8. What are you doing?
9. What are you wearing? Describe the colors.

Continue to ask questions that elicit the details you need to construct a clear visual image.

The second element of the description is SOUND.

1. Describe the tone, pitch, volume, etc.
2. What does it sound like after you have accomplished your goal?
3. What are you saying?
4. What is being said to you?
5. What are the surrounding sounds?
6. Are you being congratulated?
7. Are you being praised?

It is important that the sounds you hear be positive, constructive and reinforcing sounds that support your visualization. The sounds that accompany your visual image should be consistent and harmonious with that image. In the example of the mansion, the sounds you hear may include that of the door opening, others congratulating you for having chosen and acquired such a beautiful home, etc.

While it may be obvious that sounds should be consistent with the visual image, caution dictates that I mention the reason nonetheless. If you have a visual image of one thing and your sounds are inconsistent, your subconscious mind will become confused and, quite likely, reject the message you are trying to convey. So consistency and harmony are a must.

The third element of a sensory-rich goal description is TOUCH. In describing your goal, include what your accomplished goal feels like in the physical sense.

1. Perhaps you feel a handshake or a congratulatory pat on the back.

2. Or maybe you feel the smoothness of a champagne glass as you are toasting your success.

3. Or you may feel the knob of the door as you open it.

Describe what you would feel and experience when you realize your goal. Remember, you are constructing a sensory-rich image to be presented to the subconscious mind as though it had already been accomplished. The sense of touch is an excellent way of adding to this sense of realism. The more details you give, the more real the image will seem. While you can't visualize the actual feeling of touch, you can visualize yourself touching or being touched. This visual image, along with the mental experiences of touching, embellishes the realism of your visual image.

The fourth element is the sense of TASTE. You can imagine the taste of champagne as you are being toasted, or if you don't drink, the taste of mineral water. Develop a strong sense of taste that is consistent with your other descriptions.

The fifth element of this sensory-rich description is SMELL. It. too, should be consistent with the other descriptions.

In addition to the five senses, your description should also include your emotional reaction to having accomplished your goal. When you add all of these senses and feelings to a strong visual image, your goal is packaged in a believable way that is easily accepted by the subconscious mind.

Affirmations

Affirmations are positive statements that support and reinforce your commitment to your goal. They are one-sentence statements, given in the present tense, that trigger the mental presence of your True Purpose, True Talent and True Goal statements and their sensory-rich goal descriptions. They should use precise positive language, and be a link in a chain of consistency. Each link should support and naturally lead to the next in a logical progression.

While it is generally agreed that affirmations should be stated in the present tense, there is disagreement as to how the present tense should be stated. In the most widely published approach, the affirmation states the goal in the present tense as though it has already been accomplished. Such a statement reads:

I have a net worth of $1 million.

Other experts take the position that present tense does not mean making a statement that the mind, the conscious mind at least, knows to be untrue. The theory is that a statement like the one just given creates more disharmony between the conscious and the subconscious mind. These experts hold that statements which begin with "I can," "It can," and so on are the most conducive to harmony and are, therefore, the most effective. These experts would say:

I can have a net worth of $1 million.

This statement is clearly in the present tense because it focuses on the "I can."

I believe that, if used together, both kinds of statements can be effective. My approach is to combine the "I can" statement with the "I am" or "I have" statement. For example:

1. I have a net worth of $1 million.
2. I can see myself. . .
3. I can hear myself. . .
4. I can feel myself touching. . .
5. I can taste. . .
6. I can smell. . .
7. I have a net worth of $1 million.

One of the most knowledgeable experts in the field of subliminal messages believes the "I can" statements are the best vehicles. But in reviewing my tapes, he stated that he felt that my approach of using both "I can" and "I am" or "I have" statements was effective and powerful.

When you write your affirmations, I suggest that you use my method of combining both the "I can" and "I am" or "I have" statements.

THREE
EMPOWERING YOUR
PERSONAL GOALS

APPLYING THE TECHNIQUES

Merging Your True Purpose, True Talent and True Goal with the Empowering Process of Sensory Rich Goal Setting

You are now ready to move from the empowering stage to the creating stage. Up to this point, you have learned about True Purpose, True Talent and True Goal, focusing on their philosophical and theoretical aspects, and you have learned the theories and techniques of empowering your goal. This section is a practicum in which you will write your sensory-rich descriptions and affirmations.

Turn to page 206 to the worksheet entitled, "A True Purpose Sensory-Rich Description" and complete the exercise. If you feel that your True Purpose has changed, write what you think it is now. Remember, your True Purpose is a general statement that contains several possible goals.

If your True Purpose is to be a leader and your True Goal is to be politician, the SIGHT portion of your True Purpose description may look like this:

> I see myself standing on a podium before a large crowd, speaking into a microphone. I see them applauding my speech, and I see myself stepping off the platform and going into the crowd, shaking hands, being patted on the back and congratulated. I see them smiling and congratulating me on the wonderful, influential and moving speech that I have just given.

In the space provided under SIGHT, using approximately 75 words, describe what living your True Purpose looks like. Describe its size, shape, color, action, etc. A word of caution: The description of your True Purpose will be more general than your True Goal description which will be detailed and specific. However, your descriptions will overlap. Some of the details in your True Purpose description may show up in your True Talent or your True Goal descriptions.

If, for example, your True Goal is to be a politician within your True Purpose of leadership, your True Goal description would look like this:

> I see myself standing before a vast crowd and giving a *political* speech. I am seeking *political* office and am being *endorsed and supported* by the people there, etc.

You can see from this example that your True Goal sensory description is much more specific than your True Purpose sensory description.

Next is SOUND. Describe the sounds you would hear as you visualize the things you have described under sight. For example, if your visualization under sight was that of a leader speaking to an audience, then the sounds would possibly include the cheering of the audience, the applause, the congratulations of the people as you move through the crowd, and the sound of the slap on the back, etc.

For TOUCH, describe the touches you would experience as you do the things you have described in your sight and sound descriptions. Perhaps you feel the cool smoothness of the podium as you grip it. Or you may feel the sweat running off your forehead as you talk. Maybe you can feel the roughness, smoothness, or softness of the hands that you shake, or the firmness of the pats on the back as you go through the crowd. Write a clear description of the touches you would make and receive in this situation.

For SMELL, describe the smells that you would experience as you do the things you described in the sight and sound descriptions. In our example, you may be outside speaking to the crowd so you would smell the trees, the fresh air, and as you move through the crowd, perhaps you would smell the people's cologne or perfume. The more detailed your descriptions, the better.

The next category is TASTE. Describe what you would experience in terms of taste as you do the things that you described in the sight, sound, touch and smell descriptions. Perhaps you would taste the salty sweat coming off your face. Or taste the juice or water that is on the podium for you to drink. Maybe you would kiss babies and taste the milk on their cheeks. Be as imaginative as you can.

Now go quickly to the EMOTIONS section and write what you feel when you do the things in your sight, sound, touch, smell and taste descriptions. Do you feel a sense of direction. Do you feel a sense of direction, a sense of destiny? Do you feel at ease, relaxed, determined, happy, committed, confident? Do you feel self-esteem and the satisfaction of helping someone? Perhaps you feel satisfaction and elation as the crowd applauds you. Or you may feel the depth of your commitment as you describe an issue. Maybe you feel joy, love, and sensitivity as you go through the crowd of people who are expressing their appreciation for you.

Write your own description now. Give it the details that suit you. Remember the purpose of the description is to aid you in creating a sensory-rich vision of your goal.

A TRUE PURPOSE SENSORY-RICH DESCRIPTION

My True Purpose is...

Describe your True Purpose (use 75 words or less in each category):

SIGHT...

SOUND...

TOUCH...

SMELL...

TASTE...

EMOTIONS...

TRUE PURPOSE AFFIRMATIONS

Write affirmations that support and trigger your True Purpose sensory-rich description.

My True Purpose is. . .

Describe your True Purpose:

I am or I have. . .

I can see myself. . . .

I can hear myself. . . .

I can feel myself. . .

I can smell. . .

I can taste...

I can feel...

I am or I have...

TRUE TALENT SENSORY-RICH DESCRIPTION

Write your True Talent in a manner that supports and connects to your True Purpose, but with emphasis on the realization and the use of your True Talent. For example, if your True Purpose is to eliminate hunger and your True Talent is that of influencing and persuading people, then your description should include using your True Talent under circumstances and conditions aimed toward your True Purpose. of eliminating hunger.

My True Talent is. . .

Describe your True Talent (use 75 words or less in each category):

SIGHT. . .

SOUND. . .

TOUCH. . .

SMELL. . .

TASTE. . .

EMOTIONS. . .

TRUE TALENT AFFIRMATIONS

My True Talent is...

Describe your True Talent:

I am or I have...

I can see myself....

I can hear myself....

I can feel myself...

I can smell...

I can taste...

I can feel...

I am or I have...

True Goal Sensory-Rich Description

Now that you have completed the True Purpose Sensory-Rich Description and the True Talent Sensory-Rich Description, you have integrated your True Purpose and your True Talent. You are now ready to develop a sensory-rich goal statement. Your objective is to describe your True Goal in a way that integrates your True Purpose and uses your True Talent to accomplish that purpose.

Using our example again, if your True Purpose is to eliminate hunger and your True Talent is that of persuading and influencing people, then your True Goal may be to become a politician. Your True Goal Sensory-Rich Description would include components of your True Purpose and your True Talent, but would emphasize your True Goal.

The SIGHT section of your statement may look like this:

I see myself as a politician, giving speeches and writing bills aimed at accomplishing my True Purpose of eliminating hunger. I see myself using my talent of speaking and persuading as I address a large crowd of people who have the power to eliminate hunger. I see myself talking to corporate executives and heads of governments. I see myself addressing the United Nations.

Now take a few minutes and write your True Goal Sensory-Rich Description. Remember to include all five senses plus your emotional responses. After you have finished, write affirmations that support your True Goal. (See the True Goal Affirmations worksheet on page 215.)

TRUE GOAL SENSORY-RICH DESCRIPTION

My True Goal is. . .

Describe your True Goal (use 75 words or less in each category):

SIGHT. . .

SOUND. . .

TOUCH. . .

SMELL. . .

TASTE. . .

EMOTIONS. . .

TRUE GOAL AFFIRMATIONS

My True Goal is. . .

Describe your True Goal:

I am or I have. . .

I can see myself. . . .

I can hear myself. . . .

I can feel myself. . .

I can smell. . .

I can taste...

I can feel...

I am or I have...

FOUR
DEVELOPING YOUR PERSONAL
SUCCESS SCRIPT

1

SELF-TALK—DEVELOPING AFFIRMATIONS

Now that you have completed the exercises that deal with the sensory-rich descriptions, you should have a list of affirmations that support your True Purpose, your True Talent and your True Goal. Select from these affirmations the ones you want to use and then rewrite them, including the sensory component. You should include both "I can" and "I am" or "I have" statements in your affirmations.

1. Include one "I am" or "I have" affirmation at the beginning of the list, and repeat that affirmation at the end of the list.
2. In between those two "I am" or "I have" affirmations, you should have six affirmations about the same subject that state:

   - I can see myself. . .
   - I can hear myself. . .
   - I can taste. . .
   - I can feel myself. . .
   - I can smell myself. . .
   - I can feel the emotion of. . .

For each affirmation that you select, you will write eight affirmation statements. Now select at least five affirmations from each of your lists and rewrite those affirmations using this formula.

SELF-TALK—DEVELOPING VISUALIZATION IMAGES

The Key Word Exercise

The following exercise is called the Key Word Exercise. Its objective is to identify a word (or no more than four words) that triggers the sensory-rich vision of your True Purpose, True Talent and True Goal. The word(s) must be one that represents the common thread that runs through each of these subjects. The exercise is a relaxation exercise. Use the same relaxation suggestions that you recorded earlier. After you have listened to the relaxation suggestions, follow the instructions set forth below.

Recall to your mind your True Purpose as you described it earlier. Now take a deep breath and on each count from 5 to 1, relax more and more. Begin to see yourself doing the things you described in your True Purpose. What type of place is it? Are you outside, or are you inside? See yourself as you go about the activity that captures your True Purpose.

Hear others coming up to you, or hear the sounds around you as you go about your True Purpose. Are the sounds—of people, of animals, of cars, of machinery—consistent with what you visualized as your True Purpose?

Imagine the smells that are all around you. Are they consistent with your picture and your sounds?

Move on to touch, and imagine yourself feeling the things that you see in the picture. Are the things you touch consistent with the sight, sound, and smell descriptions?

Imagine how various things taste. Describe that taste in a way that is consistent with your other descriptions.

Finally, describe your emotions as you realize your True Purpose. Do you feel elation, satisfaction, euphoria, excitement or enthusiasm? Describe those emotions and see them as consistent with the sight, sound, smell, touch, and taste descriptions.

As you see yourself acting out your True Purpose, look slightly above your head and to your right. There, on a big billboard, you see your name and your True Purpose statement. As you look, you see one word in the statement that says it all; it immediately brings your entire True Purpose statement to mind. The letters in that word are becoming bolder, and it begins to move out from the rest. It may be the word *power*, or *love*, or *me*. It can be any word that you are comfortable with, but choose a word from your True Purpose that captures most what your True Purpose is. As you see or hear that word, the description of your True Purpose Sensory-Rich Description begins to play in your mind's eye. Whenever you want to bring this description to mind, say that word.

Now see your True Talent Statement on the billboard and repeat the above exercise, extracting a word that captures your True Talent. It may be the same word that appeared in your True Purpose Statement or it may be a different word that represents a common thread running through them.

When you have completed the exercise, do the same exercise for your True Goal Statement. After you have finished all three exercises, combine the words and use it, or them, in your key word affirmations.

Writing Your Key Word Affirmations

Write a statement of your True Purpose as you described it before, and under the statement write the word that triggers the recall of this statement and the descriptions. Write one "I am" or "I have" affirmation, and then write five "I can" affirmations using each of the five senses.

Repeat the "I am" or "I have" affirmation at the end. Include in your affirmation statements the key word from your True Purpose.

Now do the same thing for True Talent and True Goal.

You may want to simply rewrite your other affirmations including the key word, or you may find it better to use the previous affirmations only as a guide for writing new key word affirmations. Do what suits you best. They are for you.

Discussion

Have you been able to extract the same word from your True Purpose, your True Goal and your True Talent statements? Or did you extract more than one word? Were you able to write affirmations using that word?

Close your eyes and sit quietly for a moment. Say the word, or words, to yourself. Say it again and again. Then open your eyes.

When you said the word, or words, to yourself, did you get a clear picture, a clear vision, and go through the sensory exercise with your True Talent, your True Goal and your True Purpose?

In the future, when you want to recall this picture, simply say this word. You do not have to respond to the word unless you want to, so if someone else says the word it will not trigger a recall. But when you say it, the picture will come to mind.

SELF-TALK—SCRIPTING YOUR PERSONAL SUCCESS TAPE

Personalized Affirmations
for Subliminal and Supraliminal Tapes

This section is designed to assist you in creating personalized subliminal and supraliminal tapes. First, write five sets of affirmations, using the key word that you previously selected. In each set, the first affirmation will be "I am" or "I have," followed by five "I can" affirmations. The last one will be an "I am" or "I have" affirmation.

After you have done this, write five sets of affirmations for your True Purpose, five sets for your True Talent and five sets for your True Goal. The result should be a minimum of forty key word affirmations for each.

Test each affirmation against the rules for writing affirmations which appear in the checklist below.

☐ Write in present tense

☐ Use positive language

☐ Make a declarative sentence

☐ Write as though it has already occurred

☐ Mix "I am" or "I have" statements with "I can" statements

If your affirmations meet these requirements, write them on the page entitled "Self-Talk Script."

SELF-TALK SCRIPT

True Purpose Affirmations:

Set One:

1. I am or I have...

2. I can see..

3. I can hear...

4. I can touch...

5. I can smell...

6. I can taste...

7. I can feel...

8. I am or I have...

Set Two:

1. I am or I have...

2. I can see..

3. I can hear...

4. I can touch...

5. I can smell...

6. I can taste...

7. I can feel...

8. I am or I have...

Set Three:

1. I am or I have...

2. I can see..

3. I can hear...

4. I can touch...

5. I can smell...

6. I can taste...

7. I can feel...

8. I am or I have...

Set Four:

1. I am or I have...

2. I can see..

3. I can hear...

4. I can touch...

5. I can smell...

6. I can taste...

7. I can feel...

8. I am or I have...

Set Five:

1. I am or I have...

2. I can see..

3. I can hear...

4. I can touch...

5. I can smell...

6. I can taste...

7. I can feel...

8. I am or I have...

True Talent Affirmations:

Set One:

1. I am or I have...

2. I can see..

3. I can hear...

4. I can touch...

5. I can smell...

6. I can taste...

7. I can feel...

8. I am or I have...

Set Two:

1. I am or I have...

2. I can see..

3. I can hear...

4. I can touch...

5. I can smell...

6. I can taste...

7. I can feel...

8. I am or I have...

Set Three:

1. I am or I have...

2. I can see..

3. I can hear...

4. I can touch...

5. I can smell...

6. I can taste...

7. I can feel...

8. I am or I have...

Set Four:

1. I am or I have...

2. I can see..

3. I can hear...

4. I can touch...

5. I can smell...

6. I can taste...

7. I can feel...

8. I am or I have...

Set Five:

1. I am or I have...

2. I can see..

3. I can hear...

4. I can touch...

5. I can smell...

6. I can taste...

7. I can feel...

8. I am or I have...

True Goal Affirmations:

Set One:

1. I am or I have...

2. I can see..

3. I can hear...

4. I can touch...

5. I can smell...

6. I can taste...

7. I can feel...

8. I am or I have...

Set Two:

1. I am or I have...

2. I can see..

3. I can hear...

4. I can touch...

5. I can smell...

6. I can taste...

7. I can feel...

8. I am or I have...

Set Three:

1. I am or I have...

2. I can see..

3. I can hear...

4. I can touch...

5. I can smell...

6. I can taste...

7. I can feel...

8. I am or I have...

Set Four:

1. I am or I have...

2. I can see..

3. I can hear...

4. I can touch...

5. I can smell...

6. I can taste...

7. I can feel...

8. I am or I have...

Set Five:

1. I am or I have...

2. I can see..

3. I can hear...

4. I can touch...

5. I can smell...

6. I can taste...

7. I can feel...

8. I am or I have...

The affirmations that you have done make up your self-talk library. You should draw on this library to create the beliefs that support and lead to your success. I have recorded my self-talk script on a cassette tape that I listen to several times a day. My tape is both subliminal and supraliminal (recorded at normal volume). There is quite a bit of controversy about the effectiveness of subliminal tapes. I have found that some subliminal tapes have been effective for me and some have not. Those that worked best for me were the ones that contained affirmations that related to my personal situation. Unfortunately, these were few and far between. What I learned from this, however, is that the concept on which subliminal tapes is based is a valid one, but to be effective the tapes must be personalized to relate specifically and directly to your situation.

If you wish a personalized subliminal-supraliminal tape, mail your script along with a check for $95 to the author. He will produce a tape specifically for you, using your affirmations.

4
POWER TO CREATE

I congratulate you again! You have embarked on the exciting discovery of your True Purpose, your True Talent, and your True Goal. These will lead you to that unique life that you ought to be living. As I told you in the preface of this book, I cannot identify what your life is to be, but I have led you along the path of self-discovery.

Through the exercises in this book, you have put yourself on an invisible track that will lead you to the life you ought to be living—a life of great creativity and success.

Joseph Campbell said that when you put yourself on that invisible track, "you begin to meet people who are in the field of your bliss [your True Purpose], and they open the doors to you. I say, follow your bliss and don't be afraid, and doors will open where you didn't know they were going to be. Wherever you are—if you are following your bliss, you are enjoying that refreshment, that life within you, all the time."

You have that life within you—it's called the power to create. It's your power to create the kind of future that you want and deserve. I urge you to use this power today and start your journey to personal success.